CAR
BODYWORK
& INTERIOR
CARE & REPAIR

DAVID POLLARD

VELOCE PUBLISHING PLC
PUBLISHERS OF FINE AUTOMOTIVE BOOKS

Other books of interest to enthusiasts available from Veloce -

Alfa Romeo Tipo 6C, 1500, 1750 & 1900
by Angela Cherrett
Alfa Romeo Modello 8C 2300
by Angela Cherrett
Alfa Romeo Giulia Coupé GT & GTA
by John Tipler
Biggles!
by Peter Berresford Ellis & Jennifer Schofield
British Car Factories from 1896 - A Complete Survey
by Paul Collins & Michael Stratton
Bugatti 57 - The Last French Bugatti
by Barrie Price
Car Security Manual
by David Pollard
Citroën 2CV Family Album
by Andrea & David Sparrow
Citroën DS Family Album
by Andrea & David Sparrow

Fiat & Abarth 124 Spider & Coupé
by John Tipler
Fiat & Abarth 500/600
by Malcolm Bobbitt
Lola T70
by John STarkey
Mazda MX5/Miata Enthusiast's Workshop Manual
by Rod Grainger & Pete Shoemark
Mini Cooper: The Real Thing!
by John Tipler
Nuvolari: When Nuvolari Raced
by Valerio Moretti
Pass the MoT
by David Pollard
The Prince & I - My Life with the Motor Racing Prince of Siam (biography of racing driver 'B.Bira')
by Princess Ceril Birabongse
Standard and Standard-Triumph - The Illustrated History
by Brian Long
Total Tuning for the Classic MG Midget/A-H Sprite
by Daniel Stapleton

First published in 1994 by Veloce Publishing Plc, Godmanstone, Dorset DT2 7AE, England.
Fax: 0300 341065

ISBN 1 874105 36 7

Readers with ideas for automotive books, or books on other transport or related hobby subjects, are invited to write to the editorial director of Veloce Publishing at the above address.

British Library Cataloguing in Publication Data -
A catalogue record for this book is available from the British Library.

Typesetting (Avant Garde, 7/9) design and page make-up all by Veloce on AppleMac.

Printed and bound in England.

CONTENTS

ACKNOWLEDGEMENTS

The following companies provided useful help and/or information and photos for this book:

• Auto-K, 2 Daimler Close, Royal Oak Industrial Estate, Daventry, Northants, NN11 5QJ. (0327 72111)
• Automaxi Ltd., Chiltern Trading Estate, Grovebury Road, Leighton Buzzard, Beds, LU7 8TU. (0525 383131)
• Auto-plas Ltd., 90 Main Road, Hawkwell, Hockley, Essex, SS5 4JH. (0702 202795)
• Autostyle Unique Carpet Sets, Suite 1 & 2, The Barn, Hilltop Business Park, Devizes Road, Salisbury, Wilts. SP3 4UF. (0722 330809)
• BBS, Magard Ltd., 372 East Park Road, Leicester, LE5 5AY. (0533 730831)
• Black & Decker Ltd., West Point, The Grove, Slough, Berks, SL1 1QQ. (0753 511234)
• Comma Oils and Chemicals Ltd., Denton Industrial Area, Lower Grange Road, Gravesend, Kent. DA12 2QX. (0474 564311)
• W. David & Sons Limited (Isopon), 1 Totteridge Lane, Whetstone, London, N20 0AY. (081 445 0372)
• Gunson Ltd., Pudding Mill Lane, Stratford, London, E15 2PJ. (081 555 7421)
• Hammerite Products Limited (Waxoyl), Prudoe, Horthumberland, NE42 6LP. (0661 830000)
• Hella Ltd., Wildmere Road Estate, Banbury, Oxon, OX16 7JU. (0295 272233)
• Holt Lloyd Ltd (Turtle Wax), Lloyds House, Aldersley Road, Wilmslow, Cheshire, SK9 1QT. (0625 526838)
• Humbrol Ltd., Marfleet, Hull, HU9 5NE. (0482 701191)
• Kent Chamois Company, PO Box 16, Tunbridge Wells, Kent, TN3 0JZ. (0892 740563)
• Loctite UK, Welwyn Garden City, Herts, AL7 1JB. (0707 331277). (Special thanks go to Loctite who provided much of the information for Chapter 4. You can obtain their useful leaflets, *Making glue work for you* and *The good glue guide* directly from them at the address above. For 'sticky' problems, contact their technical helpline on the number given.
• Metro Products Ltd., 98-102 Station Road East, Oxted, Surrey, RH8 0AY. (0883 717644)
• Otley Trading Ltd., 8 Henley Road, Rakegate, Wolverhampton, Staffs, WV10 6UY. (0902 784693)
• Securon Ltd, Winchmore Hill, Amersham, Bucks, HP7 0NZ. (0494 434455)
• Sykes-Pickavant Tools Ltd., Warwick Works, Kilnhouse Lane, Lytham St Annes, Lancs, FY8 3DU. (0253 721291)
• Teng Tools, Tengvise Ltd., Unit 5, Flitwick Industrial Estate, Maulden Road, Flitwick, Beds, MK45 1UF. (0525 718080)
• Warco Benches, Warren Machine Tools (Guildford) Ltd, Warren Court, Middle Street, Shere, Surrey. (048 841 3434)
• Yardey Products Ltd. (Rokee), Unit 6, The Union Centre, Hillbottom, High Wycombe, Bucks, HP12 4HN. (0494 472966)

My thanks also to:
Sony (UK) Ltd., who provided a CCD-FX700E Hi-8 camcorder which was used as a video notebook and made collating facts and procedures so much easier.
Phil Blundell and Jeremy Redman of PMB Mobile Servicing (0908 504229/0374 290850), for providing skill and ingenuity in equal amounts.
As ever, thanks to Ann for for her patience in checking and collating and Bill Everitt for some cold weather patience!
All original diagrams by Davan Designs, 16, Willow Way, Wing, Bucks LU7 0TJ.

SAFETY
IMPORTANT SAFETY PROCEDURES

The rewards for the DIY motorist are many, not least of which is saving money. It's important, however, to ensure that it doesn't cost you dear in other areas - whenever you are working on your car, personal safety - and that of anyone else involved - is paramount.

By definition, a motor car is an inherently dangerous beast, even when it's stationary. For example, there are around 20 fatalities every year involving jacks, ramps or axle stands. The 'injuries' list - burns, bruises, asphyxia, fractures and crushing - is much longer. Follow these simple tips, apply a little common sense and you'll make your motoring life easier, safer and a lot less painful.

❑ PERSONAL PROTECTION
Always protect your eyes - you only get one pair! When you're working under the car, there's the constant likelihood of rust and dirt falling around you and spray paint or underseal is not designed to work like eye drops! If you don't wear goggles, you could seriously damage your eyesight. Even if, like me, you wear glasses, there are goggles available which protect the eyes but still allow you to see straight! You should also wear eye protection when using machinery (such as electric drills, sanders, grinders, etc.) likely to produce airborne detritus.

It's also a good idea to wear gloves when performing many of the tasks shown here. Plastic gloves, when dealing with strong glues, provide a 'safety net' in case of a moment's mishandling and they should also be used during paint spraying/ undersealing operations. Use strong gloves to protect your hands when you're tackling corrosion problems where there are likely to be slivers of rusted metal around and/or when you're using powerful electronic machinery. Gardening gloves are generally OK, but you should note that those with a cloth backing are totally un-

Protecting your hands and eyes is essential: use a mask when sanding, spraying or using harmful chemicals.

suitable for welding/brazing work as they could easily catch fire.

❑ BREATHE EASILY
For many of the bodywork jobs described; sanding down, spraying, using thinners, you'll be adding something to the atmosphere. Work in the open wherever possible or in a well ventilated workshop. If there's any danger of breathing in anything other than clean, fresh air, wear a mask of the sort sold in packs at most DIY stores.

❑ RAISING THE CAR
If you need to raise the car (in order to get at underbody rust, for example) extreme care is required. Ideally, use a suitable trolley jack to raise the car; at a push, use the vehicle's wheel-changing jack, but remember that it will be nowhere near as capable as a trolley jack because it was designed for emergencies only and not for supporting the weight of the car for long periods of time. Whatever you do, **NEVER, EVER** get underneath a car, or even work

Wherever possible, use a trolley jack to raise your car and ...

on its perimeter, when it is supported only by a jack of any description - even a trolley jack.

If it is not possible to use ramps, use axle stands to take the weight of the car over a period of time. Unless the job you are doing necessitates otherwise, leave the hand-

... then support it using axle stands or ramps to keep it safely there.

Squarely on the ramps, handbrake on, in first gear with wheels chocked. Perfect!

brake on and the car in a low gear, and **ALWAYS** chock the wheels still on the ground.

❑ FIRE
Working with flammable materials makes a fire extinguisher - and the ability to use it - highly desirable. A small spark or flame may be all that's required to set light to your car or, of course, that tank full of petrol. According to AA calculations, the energy stored in the average fuel tank is enough to blow a car a mile high!

• Don't forget - **NEVER** put water on an engine fire.

❑ GLUES
Modern glues are highly effective and especially useful when working with your car's trim, **BUT** they must be handled with caution simply *because* of their efficiency. Al-

ways read the instructions on the pack. For further details about this sticky subject, see the Chapter on Glues.

A fire extinguisher is essential for any workshop, especially when working with paints and thinners, etc.

❏ PAINTS AND THINNERS

It's a good idea to use plastic gloves when you're painting or spraying or using thinners as a cleaner: some paints can only be washed out of brushes, etc., by using thinners (rather than white spirit). Make sure that you put the thinners in a suitable container and store away from tiny hands.

If you're dismantling trim where electrical wires may be disturbed, disconnect the battery earth terminal first.

Talking of hands, if you do manage to get paint or resins on your hands, Loctite's PARR (paint and resin remover) hand cleaner is an excellent way to get them clean. It's formulated with a mild, safe cleaning agent (DBE) and is non-combustible and biodegradable. Technically, automotive bodyshops are now required to lower the number of volatile organic compounds (VOC) used. PARR's VOC is 5.5% compared to 50-100% in other products used for similar purposes. In everyday terms, it gets rid of the paint without adversely affecting your skin in the way that many harsher cleaners do.

❏ SAFETY HINTS & TIPS

• Whenever you are working on your car, remove the ignition key and put the car in gear with the handbrake on.

• Coat your hands with barrier cream before you start any dirty work. It makes them easier to clean when you finish and helps offset the detrimental affects of oil and grease on the skin.

• Do not allow children to play in or around a car you are working on.

• Do not smoke (or allow others to) when you are working on your car, especially if you are working with paints, thinners, etc.

• If you need to check items beneath the car, make sure it cannot move; put the car in a low gear and the handbrake on. As a 'belt and braces' measure, chock the front and rear wheels.

• Whenever you are working on your car (and particularly if you are working under it) it's a good idea to have a helper on hand - even if it's only for moral support. Failing that, make sure that someone knows

Thinners for washing brushes should be stored in a screw cap container and kept away from children.

This locking cupboard is ideal for storing dangerous chemicals and sprays.

where you are and checks on you occasionally (if you're lucky, it will be an opportunity for a coffee break!).

• **NEVER** run your engine in the confines of your garage, always work outdoors. Exhaust fumes can kill within minutes, even if they've passed through a catalytic converter.

• If you're working in the engine bay, do so with a cool (preferably cold) engine. Remember that many modern cars have electric cooling fans which switch on thermostatically several minutes after the engine has been switched off - keep your fingers and clothing out of the way.

Getting paint and/or resins from your skin is a job for Loctite's paint and resin remover (PARR) - it does the job with far less damage to your hands than many cleaners.

TOOLS
ADVICE ON THE TOOLS YOU'LL NEED

Most of the procedures detailed in this book can be effected using tools typically found in the average DIY enthusiast's workshop.

❏ BUYING
Always buy good quality items from a respected manufacturer and get a good warranty. The cheap tools on offer at 'bargain' shops are often the manufacturers' reject castings and are likely to break under pressure.

Good tools aren't cheap, but then neither are the bits of you that are likely to be damaged as a result of tools failing to do their job. In many respects, and particularly when you're just beginning your tool collection, it's a good idea to buy sets of tools (screwdrivers, for example) rather than individual instruments.

TOOL CARE
Take care of your tools and they'll take care of you - an old adage, but true, nonetheless. Get yourself a strong tool box and keep your tools in it. Once you've finished your work, wipe your tools and put them where you'll be able to find them next time. Put power tools out of harm's way with the cable neatly wound up; put drill bits and similar accessories either in their carry cases or in a specific box of your own choosing (plastic pâté containers are ideal!).

Always clean paintbrushes as soon as you've finished with them - use water, white spirit or thinners as required.

CARRYING & STORAGE
A cantilever-style box is ideal for carrying tools around, whereas a tool chest is designed to be more of a permanent fixture. Initial cost dwindles to nothing when spread over a number of years.

Plastic abrasive wheels are sometimes a useful alternative to the harsher wire type for removing paint.

CHOOSING
Use the right tool for the job; obvious, but a great many DIY motorists are injured every year because they didn't obey this simple rule. Using a small screwdriver on a screw which requires a large one is a recipe for a damaged screw head, a damaged car and possibly damaged fingers!

❏ POWER TOOLS
The purchase of power tools for use on your car can usually be justified in that they can also be used for home DIY jobs. Of these, an electric drill is possibly the single most useful power tool you can have. Ideally, go for a variable speed model with some real oomph - 500W or more output. That way, it will be able to stand up to just about everything you can throw at it, including sanding and wire brushing operations, as described later.

A cordless drill should be next on your list. They are physically smaller and, having no mains cable or extension to get in the way, gain in versatility what they lose in sheer power output. Most have a slow enough speed setting to be used as an electric screwdriver, too.

Not as powerful, but its versatility makes the cordless drill a welcome addition to any workshop.

A jigsaw is very useful when working on bodywork and trim - note the protective guard in position.

If you do a lot of DIY, a purpose-made electric screwdriver will soon earn its keep, especially when you remember that motor manufacturers love fixing their cars together with crosshead self-tapping screws.

If you can justify the investment (for such it is) an electric jigsaw makes light work of trim modifications such as making holes for speakers.

❏ SAFETY FIRST

It's important to remember that all power tools are inherently dangerous: respect them at all times and you'll have a long and happy relationship.

When using a mains powered item, consider the routing of the electrical lead; will it pass through a puddle? Or an oil patch? Can the wire be trapped (and possibly cut) by a closed door?

EYES AND HANDS

Many jobs involving power tools offer an opportunity to try out your thick gloves and goggles; the latter especially should be worn whenever there is the slightest possibility of airborne detritus, for your eyes cannot be replaced and it's so easy to dam-

This spray gun is ideal for painting larger areas, particularly interior trim.

age them beyond repair.

If you are using your drill as a sander or powered wire brush (with suitable attachments), you may need to wear a mask to prevent breathing in noxious substances.

EXTERNAL TRIM
TECHNIQUES FOR REMOVING AND FITTING EXTERNAL TRIM

❏ **EXTERIOR TRIM REMOVAL AND FITTING**
For many bodywork procedures you'll have the problem of what to do about the decorative trim. If you're spraying, it is sometimes possible to mask it off, but it's usually better to remove it. It's very much the modern way for manufacturers to glue trim into place wherever possible so it's important to make a thorough examination before you start prising away in the mistaken belief that the trim piece clips into place! If you are faced with glued trim, the simplest removal method is to use a hair dryer (to melt the glue), a suitable implement to gently 'tease' it away and a large dose of patience. Bear in mind that many, apparently insignificant, badges and trim pieces cost far more than they ought to. Such items can usually be stuck back in place by using double-sided 'stickies', available from most accessory stores. When doing so, it's important to make sure that the surface is clean and grease-free - wipe over with white spirit before applying the sticky tab. Take care to get the positioning exactly right as they tend to stick first time.

Many trim items are clipped into place. Again, patience is required, as you work your way along until you find the fastener and then gently ease the trim away from it. Where you're dealing with a metal trim piece (as is often used down the flanks of a car) take great care not to bend it - you'll find it hard to get rid of the crease you make. If you're removing several trim pieces, it's a good idea to wrap a piece of masking tape around each and use a ball point pen to denote which bit is which and which way round it goes.

Some cars have trim pieces which feature bayonet-type fittings that slot into plastic inserts in the bodywork. Again, they should pry out quite easily if you're patient; it's easy to damage the trim and/or bodywork by hurrying.

The plastic inserts are often a cause of rusting so, having taken off the trim, make

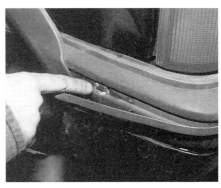

This bumper insert clips into fastenings along its edge and ...

... is secured at either end by a self-tapping screw under the wheelarch.

a thorough check to ensure there isn't a little hole working away at being a big hole!

❏ **EXTERIOR STRIPES REMOVAL AND FITTING**
The main reason for adding stripes to your car is to improve the appearance. Alternatively, it could be you had to remove an existing stripe in order to perform other work - a spot of spraying, perhaps. Either

Many plastic trim pieces feature lugs which pass through the bodywork and are secured by tags on the underside. Take your time and don't rush the job and damage the trim. The S-P trim removal tool is the Swiss Army Knife of the bodywork trade.

Use masking tape to note where each piece of trim belongs.

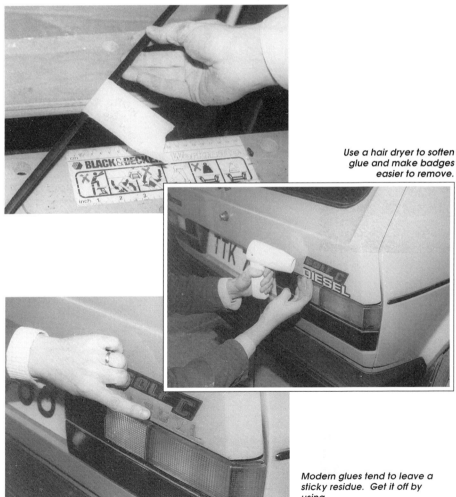

Use a hair dryer to soften glue and make badges easier to remove.

Modern glues tend to leave a sticky residue. Get it off by using ...

... white spirit. Where it is reluctant to come off ...

... we found the plastic scraper supplied with Isopon filler useful to ease it off.

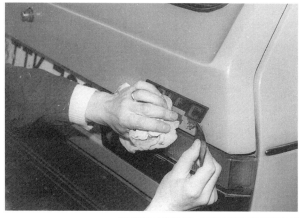

Make sure that the area for a stripe or decal is grease-free. A cutting agent will do the job well.

Adding body graphics will individualise your car - and it doesn't just have to be simple stripes.

The area to be 'striped' should be totally clean and grease-free. Thoroughly wet it with warm soapy water - when you apply the stripe, this mixture allows you to move it around to exactly the right position. When you've got it straight, use a squeegee (or credit card) to get rid of all the air bubbles that accumulate.

way, the procedure starts with getting the stripe in a straight line and following an existing line in the bodywork is the easiest method. Where there isn't one suitable, measure the position of the stripe at several points along its length and mark with pieces of masking tape. You can then fit the stripe to these points and remove the masking tape when the stripe is dry.

If you have a stripe, or body graphic, which is peeling at the edges, you can encourage it to stay in place by dabbing the very edge with a spot of clear nail varnish which will act as a gentle glue.

If you need to remove a stripe, use a heat source (hair dryer or hot air gun) to soften the glue, then ease it away.

GLUES
CHOOSING AND USING ADHESIVES

Once upon a time, glue was glue and, with it, you either constructed model aeroplanes or stuck photos in an album. The thought of using liquid adhesives to bond metal to glass or other such dissimilar materials was absurd. Not any more, and it's now common to find adhesive taking the place of nuts, bolts, rivets and welding in all manner of manufacturing processes. And don't let's forget either that many sections of modern Formula One cars are 'glued' together!

❏ SAFETY
It is vital to be extremely careful when handling any form of adhesive, especially some of the latest 'superglues'. Many set within seconds and, by definition, are extremely reluctant to come unstuck. Getting glued fingers apart after is often a lengthy and painful process.

SOLVENT ABUSE
The dangers of solvent abuse are known to most of us which is why it's vital that powerful adhesives are kept safely under lock and key.

CHILDREN
ALWAYS, always store glues out of the reach of children. If you've got a lockable bench cupboard like mine, this is ideal for storing poisonous and dangerous materials.

FIRE
By its very nature, glue is flammable - in a big way. Don't smoke (or allow anyone else to) when you're working with glue and make sure that there are no other naked flames around (a gas soldering iron, for example). Electricity, too, can create the spark required to start a fire. As ever, keep your fire extinguisher handy.

STICKY FINGERS
If you do stick your fingers together, DON'T PANIC - put them quickly into a bowl of hot, soapy water which should soften the glue. Keep the fingers in the water and gently prise apart with a spoon handle. As already mentioned, it's likely to be a long process, so be patient.

GLUE ON CLOTHING
If you get a drop of glue on your clothing, soak the area in nail varnish remover or acetone (both available from the chemist). Check first that the clothing is colour fast as both chemicals are extremely strong. Remember that acetone is highly toxic and flammable; keep away from naked flames or sources of ignition and do not inhale.

STUCK ON YOU
When you've got glue where it shouldn't be you need to use something like Loctite's Detach glue remover. It will remove traces of glue (including superglues) from stained surfaces, badly bonded objects, clothes, fabrics and skin. Always try out on a hidden area before applying in earnest. Where it is being used to free sticky fingers, as little as possible should be used and the skin washed with copious amounts of water as soon as possible.

CHOOSING
The latest crop of adhesives are extremely powerful and effective and they aren't cheap. They can be particularly cost-effective, however, if you buy the right one for your purposes. The choice of glues is wide, and each has a specific role in life, so there's really no excuse for buying a glue that's not suitable for the job. Read the labels carefully before you buy and ask for advice if you're still not sure.

❏ BASIC PROCEDURES
The basic rule when glueing anything to anything else revolves around one word - CLEAN! No glue works well on dirty surfaces and, although some may appear to work, they will not be performing at their best and

Using Lock 'n' Seal ensures this gear knob will now stay in place.

there's always the risk that you will, literally, come unstuck. Eliminate contamination by using acetone or nail-varnish remover, but test them first to ensure suitability.

Roughen the surfaces to be glued by using emery or wet-and-dry paper to provide a 'key' and wipe off any dust before applying the glue. All glues need time to develop full strength - most will achieve handling strength quickly or, in some cases, instantly. It's advisable to handle all glued parts with some care for at least an hour afterwards, remembering that the colder it is, the longer it takes the glue to cure.

TOO MUCH OF A GOOD THING
Modern glues are particularly efficient and you gain nothing by using too much - all you do is slow down the setting process, make everything messier than it need be and wasting money.

STORAGE
It's best to keep small tubes of glue standing upright (*i.e.*, with the nozzle at the top) so that the glue flows away from the nozzle. Special dispensers (like Loctite's Gluematic) should be stored with the nozzle at the bottom, which keeps the valve wet and working.

Use Detach to remove glue from badly bonded objects, clothes and skin, but take heed of the safety warnings.

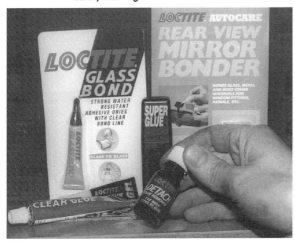

WHAT'S THE GAP?
The gap between the parts to be glued will decide which glue should be used. Where it is;

a) the thickness of a cigarette paper it's OK to use a superglue.

b) the thickness of heavy writing paper requires something slightly different such as Super Glue Gel Xtra or Multi Bond.

c) the thickness of the glue pack card will require something like Tough Bond.

❑ HINTS & TIPS
• If the area over which you need to spread the glue is large (the size of the palm of your hand, for example) you'll need to use a glue that won't go 'off' before you've finished spreading (Tough Bond or Multi Bond).

• If you are glueing parts which have to align, use a chinagraph pencil to assist accuracy.

• Don't move the parts once the glue has started to set (*i.e.*, go 'off').

• All glues take longer to work in colder conditions. Where you need it to work quickly, warm the parts to be glued to room temperature before applying the glue.

• If you're glueing in a tricky area, use masking tape to prevent the glue going where you don't want it.

• If you need to hold something temporarily (say, a small screw on the end of a screwdriver in an awkward to get at place) use a dab of Super Glue 3. Once the screw is in place, pushing the screwdriver to one side will break the bond between them.

• How will the glued parts be used after sticking? Does the joint need to be waterproof, flexible, heat-resistant, or able to withstand rough handling? Whatever your requirements, you should check on the pack before you buy the glue that you are getting exactly what you require.

• If the parts to be stuck have to be moved after the glue has been applied, choose one which stays 'workable' so that the parts can be manoeuvred.

• For slower glues, hold the parts to be joined together using masking tape or, for bigger pieces, clamps. However, don't clamp too hard or you'll squeeze the glue out altogether!

EXTERIOR VALETING
TECHNIQUES FOR KEEPING YOUR CAR 'SHOWROOM' FRESH

Looking after your car's bodywork is something you can do every week of the year simply by taking part in the time-honoured British weekend practice of 'Washing the Car'. It's not just vanity that makes this a good practice: cleaning off all that mud and road dirt allows you to see what's going on underneath and prevents it from forming a rust-cultivating poultice. If, during the course of your cleaning, you discover a rusty spot or paintwork damage, you can attend to it sooner, rather than later, preventing a minor problem becoming a major one.

❏ ASSEMBLE YOUR TOOLS
There is plenty of cleaning equipment around, so invest in some good quality gear and it should last for many years and repay its initial cost many times. Holts, for example, produce a range of brushes and accessories which can be purchased individually or as a kit.

Using decent cleaning cloths and dusters also makes life easier; that piece of rag from under the sink is likely to replace the dirt with a thousand bits of cloth fibres. Kent Chamois have a wide variety of cleaning cloths and, not surprisingly, chamois available. A good lint-free cloth is essential when you're waxing and

Holts cleaning equipment; two bodywork brushes, a lance, a hose connector and a wheel brush.

By using a special adaptor the lance and brushes can be connected to your garden hose.

polishing and a chamois (real and synthetic, depending on your taste) is the only way to get streak-free bodywork and glass.

WET WET WET
Always rinse off the car before you start cleaning in earnest. If you don't there's the danger that you'll drag along caked-on dirt and scratch the paintwork. Start at the top and work down, for obvious reasons. If you haven't got a hose, take a bucket of clean water and drip it over the car; extravagant folk have two buckets, one for rinsing and one for washing. Don't bother with the wheels yet - they're a law unto themselves and have to be treated as such.

Play the hose under the wheelarches to remove some of the build-up of road dirt. It's here where the rust bug can breed almost unhindered - particularly in the lip of the arch - and where the welder's torch is most often required. If you have plastic protective panels under your arches, remove them once in a while and make sure all is well below. While removed, it's a good idea to treat the (hopefully) pristine area to a coating of Waxoyl - you can't be too careful!

It's a good idea, say three or four times a year, to pop down to the local Jetwash and give the underneath of your car a re-

A selection of the Kent Chamois range of cleaning materials.

ally good blasting. Those things produce massively more pressure than your average garden hose and, compared with the cost of welding repairs, it's a couple of pounds well spent.

You'll need something with which to apply the shampoo/water mix - some prefer a sponge, some a brush, others a cloth -

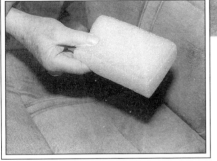

One side of this small sponge has a scourer type finish - ideal for removing flies from the windscreen.

there are benefits and drawbacks to each. Personally, I use a sponge for the larger body panels (bonnet, wings, doors etc.) but a brush to get into the awkward nooks and crannies.

SHAMPOO

Don't clean your car with washing-up liquid!! Use a purpose-made car shampoo mixed in the required proportions in a bucket of warm (not too hot) water.

Though washing-up liquid may *appear* to be having the desired effect (*i.e.* cleaning the car), in fact, it has exactly the opposite: it is designed to re-

move grease from pots and pans and, as polish is a form of grease, it does just the same here!

Many folk just use one bucketful of water/shampoo for the whole car, but it follows that if your car is dirty, it won't be long before you're applying water, shampoo and dirt. Be generous and expect to use two or even three buckets every wash. When it comes to shampoos, make a selection of the most well-known names (who have a reputation to uphold) and try them. Find the one that suits you best and stick to it - everyone has their favourites. Holts Hot Wax is an interesting idea which enables you to wash and apply a thick wax to your car at the same time.

Start washing at the top, working from

In particular, spray under the wheelarches, where mud can stick and create rust problems.

Getting thick mud off the bottom of doors reveals plenty of rust areas which would otherwise be hidden.

the roof to a line level with the trim strip partway down the doors. Then move to the other side of the car and repeat the operation, including the bonnet and tailgate/boot lid. This way, you're not transferring dirt from the much dirtier lower part of the car to the upper part. As mentioned earlier, when you find the water becoming a muddy colour and/or when there's plenty of grit in it, throw it away (not over the car!) and get a fresh bucketful.

WHEELS

Washing the wheels should be treated as a separate job, largely because they get so dirty. Use a fresh bucket of shampoo solu-

tion and, as with the bodywork, start by rinsing off first.

It is usually the case that the rear wheels will clean up very well by using shampoo solution and elbow grease. Use a strong-bristled brush and, for awkward areas, a purpose-made wheel brush.

Most cars don't have rear wheel disc brakes (and the front brakes on any car work harder anyway) which tends to keep them cleaner (or at least less likely to be affected by brake dust). But the front wheels are usually much harder to clean because the dust from the brake pads gets onto them. This requires only a little moisture to make a nasty, staining 'ink' which is very difficult to get off. The longer you leave it, the more reluctant it is to leave its happy home and the greater the danger of it permanently staining the surface. Solve this problem by using a proprietary wheel cleaner (most work on alloy or steel wheels). You'll have to work the liquid well into the wheel pattern; a specific wheel cleaning brush is ideal and, for really awkward to get at areas, an old toothbrush may be useful.

Holts Quick Wash reverses the usual procedure - you spray the shampoo directly onto the car.

Those brushes come in handy for getting into awkward nooks and crannies.

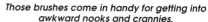

Above left: Even after being rinsed, the brake dust stains still remain on this alloy wheel.

Above right: Clean stains off by spraying with wheel cleaning solution and ...

Right: ... working it well into affected areas.

Below left: This Holts brush can be connected to the hose, allowing rinsing and brushing at the same time.

Below right: It's the same wheel - honest!

BBS wheel owners will know this technique well ... Rinsing removes the cleaner and the brake dust in one go. Most alloy wheels have a protective coating to stop corrosion, so don't be tempted to try and remove stains with abrasives.

The tyres need washing at the same time as your car's wheels and in the same way - plenty of water and effort with a stiff brush. Whilst you're down at the corners of your car, take the opportunity to check that the treads are wearing evenly with no splits or cracks and that they contain no foreign bodies. Run a visual check on your wheels, too; signs of heavy 'kerbing' damage, which can cause dangerous cracks, and general security.

You can apply a tyre wall black, though opinion as to the overall effect is divided; some say it completes the picture, others that it gives a somewhat 'Arthur Daly' impression. It's up to you! Alternatively, products like ArmorAll and Son of a Gun work well.

NO STREAKING

Once you've finished splashing about with the hose, it's time to chamois the bodywork. It's tempting just to let it air dry, but this will leave unsightly streaks on the body and irritating marks on the glass. Use a chamois to mop up the remaining water. Cheap chamois should be avoided like the plague; they'll start to 'moult' and leave bits all over your paintwork sooner rather than later. Most cleaning materials suppli-

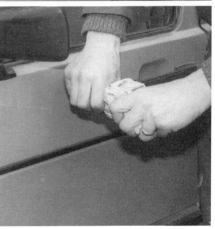

Above top: WRONG! Never wring out a chamois like this - you'll ruin it in no time.

Above: RIGHT! Squeeze out the excess water and it will last for years.

Use a chamois to wipe off excess water and prevent streaking. Start at the top and work down, rinsing the chamois regularly.

ers offer 'real' chamois leathers or synthetics - it's up to you and, in truth, there's little to choose in their effectiveness. Kent Chamois recommend that real chamois are kept moist.

GLASS
Washing and rinsing your car rarely gets the glass really clean. Use a proprietary glass cleaner - spray it on and wipe it off as described in the instructions. The glass, especially the windscreen, tends to collect a film of dust, grease, oil, diesel, rubber and insects - glass cleaners contain agents which will lift this off.

Use a lint-free cloth or, as Holts suggest, a piece of kitchen towel to wipe it off.

☐ CARING FOR YOUR CAR'S PAINTWORK
When it comes to keeping paintwork in tip-top condition, you're spoilt for choice - the variety of products available is mind-boggling. But why should this be necessary?

When a car is new, the paint surface shines like the proverbial new pin. As it gets older, the paintwork starts to look dull and faded. This is the result of the actions of the climate, the weather and wear and tear of everyday driving - chips, marks, scrapes and atmospheric pollution.

When it leaves the factory, the sheen a new car displays is high because the paint layer is (or should be!) totally smooth. If your car's paintwork looks dull, even after it's been thoroughly washed, it's because that paint layer is pitted and rough.

The diagram alongside shows

what a very close-up view of your car's paint surface will look like after a few years' exposure to the elements and not enough waxing.

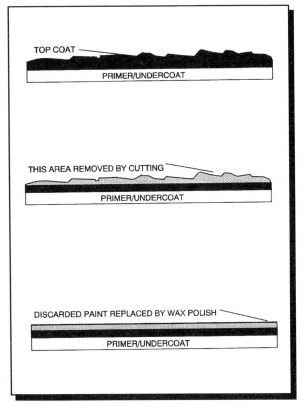

TOP COAT

PRIMER/UNDERCOAT

THIS AREA REMOVED BY CUTTING

PRIMER/UNDERCOAT

DISCARDED PAINT REPLACED BY WAX POLISH

PRIMER/UNDERCOAT

Rough top surface won't reflect the light and therefore won't shine. Using a cutting agent removes this coat and applying wax polish restores the shine and protects remaining paintwork.

CUTTING COMMENTS

If your dry, clean car is as dull as ditch water, it means that the effects of oxidisation* and not enough regular waxing have taken their toll. A spot of cutting is called for, using one of many proprietary cutting compounds on the market - reputation is your best guide. By doing this you are actually removing the top (thin) layer of paint to reveal the pristine layer below. By definition, you shouldn't cut back too often, otherwise you'll be polishing bare metal! Try the compound on paintwork out of sight (inside the boot, for example) to test for effect before you slap it on all over the bonnet.

*The adverse reaction of paint to the oxygen in the air.

When you consider how much your car cost, a quality polish is a small price to pay to protect your investment.

STRICTLY FOR THE BIRDS

You'll know the old truism that as soon as you've cleaned your car, a passing bird will 'baptise' it from a great height. However, these deposits are more than unsightly and inconvenient - they are actually very corrosive and should be removed as soon as possible to prevent lasting damage to the paint surface. Moreover, the longer anything sticks to the body of your car, the greater the danger that area will appear a different colour when it is eventually cleaned off.

Spraying polish directly onto your cloth prevents it getting onto glass or other trim.

❏ POLISHING

Polishing is an essential part of caring for your car's body. By applying an extra layer of protection, you can help defend it against the rigours that driving subject it to; rain, sun, massive temperature differences, gravel and mud all combine to give that paintwork a hard time.

Despite some manufacturers' claims that their polishes can be applied in bright sunlight, it's always better to work in the shade or on a cloudy day as most polishes are designed to be applied out of direct sunlight.

Almost all polishes contain a small amount of abrasive agent, designed to lift off any residual dirt, and they all leave a protective coating to guard against the affects of oxidisation.

WHICH POLISH?

Ask any ten car enthusiasts which is the best polish and you'll probably get ten different answers although the common factor is always that they choose quality products, like the ones shown here. Try a few and see which suits you best.

Always read the instructions before use; some can be used in sunlight, some can be used even if the vehicle is damp, some require polishing with a circular motion. You need to know about the product in order to get the best from it.

If your car has a metallic paint finish (which is 'softer' than standard paints), it's worth investing in a polish designed specifically for it. There are many on the market and all have a slightly less abrasive nature in deference to the different paint constitution.

The latest innovations in polishing are 'colour-coded' polishes, such as Holts Color Magic, which is designed to remove the need to cut back before applying polish to a dull paint surface. Unlike traditional polishes, it is specially formulated with urethane and coloured dyes and pigments to blend

Using a grinder/sander with a buffing wheel takes the hard work out of polishing large areas.

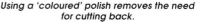

Using a 'coloured' polish removes the need for cutting back.

in with original car colours of the same general shade. An exact match is not necessary - you can choose the colour polish that most closely matches your car. It's applied in the same way as conventional polish, though it is claimed that no buffing is required and (because the polish is coloured) that there is no white residue. One application should last for 12 months.

HOW TO APPLY POLISH
Putting on polish and buffing up requires lint-free cloths - 'normal' ones will leave a polished surface covered in bits of fabric. The Kent Chamois Stockinette is ideal. Work on a section at a time; trying to wax the whole car in one go is a recipe for disaster. Keep wax polishes off glass and rubber and plastic trim. Where you're using a spray polish, spray it directly onto the cloth so that it goes where you want it to.

On large panels (the bonnet, for example) you can cheat when it comes to buffing up to a fine sheen by using a grinder/sander or an electric drill with a buffing attachment.

❏ TAR VERY MUCH
Given the way some roads are made, you're likely to find lots of nasty little black spots covering your car's bodywork, particularly in the summer road-building season. Some waxes will pull tar spots off, but it's easier to use a specific tar-removing agent. It's strong stuff, so it's important to wax over the area when you've finished.

❏ CHROME CLEANING
Time was when every car made had at least an acre of chrome to polish but, in

Use a dedicated metal polish for chrome and aluminium trim.

general, the matt-black look of the '70s has come to stay and many cars now don't feature any shiny metal at all. Where your car does have chrome, apply a spot of polish when it doesn't shine after the car has been washed and/or when you see signs of surface corrosion. The latter is usually quite simple to remove, but once the rust gets hold the chrome will become pitted and lost forever.

Autochrome is a cream that has been around a number of years with an enviable reputation not only as a chrome brightener, but also as a rust beater.

❏ ALUMINIUM TRIM
Most metal polishes can also be used on aluminium trim surfaces that don't rust as such, but suffer surface corrosion (which takes the form of a white powder). If left long enough the surface will become pitted. Clean and polish as directed and then smear a coating of light oil (or even Vaseline) over to retain the shine and prevent corrosion, especially during the winter months.

❏ CLEANING PLASTIC* BUMPERS
The trend for plastic bumpers is good in terms of improved safety and there being less chrome to rust. However, these bump-

use a small paintbrush; load the cleaner directly onto it and apply like paint. The bristles make it possible to get into every crevice in a way you can't with a cloth.

Follow the instructions on the label regarding polishing, etc. Let the cleaner dry then use a lint-free cloth to remove any excess. Some cars have grey bumpers and, you won't be surprised to learn, there's a cleaner specifically for them - use as described previously. This kind of polish can be used on most trim items of similar construction, including rubber seals. If you find that applying polish doesn't do the trick, turn to the Chapter dealing with plastic bumper spraying.

Plastic is a term used to cover most bumpers of this type, although the actual chemical compounds used vary with the manufacturer.

❏ IT'S A COVER-UP
Having spent all this time

It's easier to use a brush to apply bumper polish. Wipe off with a lint-free cloth.

and effort getting your car clean, it makes sense to try and keep it that way. If you haven't got a garage, then a car cover is the next best thing: there is the added bonus that they keep the frost from your car during cold snaps, which means clear windows and less chance of the cold thoroughly draining the battery.

❏ HINTS & TIPS
• If you value your
ers, which are usually black, have a tendency to go slightly off-colour, taking on a somewhat grey tinge with age. There are many cleaners specifically for such bumpers, though the composition of bumpers varies, so it's a good idea to try a small section first, in case there is any adverse reaction. Although the makers usually suggest that the cleaner is applied using a cloth, this means you get the stuff all over your hands in a big way, and it's like boot polish to get off - hard work. It's also tricky to get into the 'grain' of the plastic.

A far easier method of application is to
car's appearance and paintwork, I really couldn't recommend a car wash. It's quick, convenient and much in favour with company car owners (but then, the car isn't theirs), but I've yet to find one which actually does clean the whole car properly. There's also the possibility of losing an aerial or, in extreme cases, a wing mirror.

• Washing-up liquid is designed for getting grease off dishes - it performs in the same way when you use it as a 'car shampoo' - it pulls the polish off!

• Don't wash your car in bright sunlight - you'll be fighting a losing battle with

With no garage, a car cover will take care of your car. This Metro version folds into a tiny space ...

... yet expands to cover most typical saloons and hatchbacks.

This top-half cover is an alternative which will also keep the windows free from frost.

streaks and smears.

• Keep wax off all glass areas, particularly the windscreen where it can cause irritating and dangerous smearing.

• If your windscreen is smeared by polish, or just general road grime, etc., a wipe-over with newspaper will often improve the view.

• When using a spray wax, it's best to spray it directly onto the cloth, rather than the vehicle, in order to avoid messy overspray.

27

PAINTING PLASTIC BUMPERS
HOW TO GIVE YOUR CAR'S BUMPERS A NEW LEASE OF LIFE

❑ SAFETY NOTE

Whenever you are spraying and/or using potentially harmful substances (thinners, paint, etc.,) always work in a well ventilated area. Do not spend long periods of time in the presence of harmful vapours - take a break and get some fresh air, giving the nasties time to disperse.

❑ WHY BOTHER?

You may want to paint your car's bumpers (and other items of 'plastic' exterior trim) as part of a larger customising plan, but for most, it's because no amount of polishing can restore the original colour - black bumpers just get greyer every year. Many owners spray the bumpers the same colour as their cars - others opt for the contrasting look. There are many colours available, so it's up to you.

Naturally, paint spraying is much easier if you remove the bumper first. You can spray it *in situ*, but it demands some very careful masking if you are to get the paint just where you want it and not on the surrounding paintwork, glass, light lenses, etc. It's also extremely difficult to get around the very edges of the bumper.

In the example shown in this Chapter, the bumper had gone grey to the point where no amount of black trim polish would restore it. Just four, 10mm bolts needed to be undone to release the bumper.

CHECKING THE PAINT TYPE

It's important to ascertain that the paint you are using is suitable for your particular car's bumpers. Though this type of bumper is usually described as 'plastic' for ease, it isn't strictly true and the manufacturing process and component chemicals vary between manufacturers.

Before you get carried away and ruin the whole bumper - an expensive exercise - apply a little of the paint (taking note of the preparation steps listed later) to a small area on the underside of a bumper where it won't show. If there is an adverse reaction, your day's work stops there and you'll either have to find another kind of paint or forget the idea. Though most paints are sold by aftermarket suppliers, you may find that your local franchised vehicle dealer can help. However, if it goes on OK you're in business.

THE PREPARATION

As with any painting job, the workpiece (the bumper) must be clean. Give it a good wash and break a rule here - use washing-up liquid and water. Normally, this is not recommended because it pulls the wax off; in this case, that's just what you want!

Make sure that every bit of mud and dirt is removed. If your bumper has some tricky contours, use a small stiff brush or even an old toothbrush to get into those nooks and crannies. The bumper must be totally dry before you go any further: if necessary, use a hair dryer to speed up the process, especially in the intricate mouldings.

Put on your plastic gloves and wipe over the entire surface of the bumper with thinners - don't breathe this in any more than you have to and make sure there's plenty of ventilation; we completed this task with the garage door wide open! The thinners evaporates quickly and, within minutes, the bumper will be ready for spraying.

As part of your preparation, you will need masking tape and newspaper, even though the bumper is off the car. The idea is to stop over-spray covering everything else in your garage! In this case, a layer of newspaper was used as a base on the bench, with a pair of ramps, also covered in newspaper, as a backdrop. All this was secured using strips of masking tape. Because the paint in question dries so quickly, it was not necessary to devise elaborate methods of holding the bumper so that the whole thing could be sprayed in one position. It was possible to spray the top, wait

It's important to mask the surrounding area to prevent messy over-spray.

for it to air-dry, and then tip it over to work on the underside.

Note that this particular bumper had a chrome (well, plastic chrome) trim strip set into it. Removing it *was* possible, but tricky to say the least: as chrome trim has become rather old hat it was decided to spray over it. It was lightly sanded with a fine paper, after which, it was prepared in the same manner as the rest of the bumper.

THE PAINTING

We were using Humbrol's Krylon PVC spray (which can be used on other trim items) in black, though other colours are available. Like all such aerosols, it needs a good shaking before use - I'd recommend at least two minutes and more if it's a cool day.

Use the standard spraying technique; spray from around 8 inches away and keep the nozzle parallel with the bumper. Don't try and cover the surface in one go - you'll end up with a series of runs and drips. Press the button a short distance before the area you want to cover and release it after you have sprayed past the far edge of the area. Put on a number of thin coats, allowing each to touch-dry (around five minutes) first. Use gloves to prevent paint drips getting onto the skin.

When you've finished, or if you've finished one coat and are leaving it to dry thoroughly before applying another, upend the can and spray until the nozzle clears. If you don't do this, the nozzle could block up with solidified paint.

❑ REPAIRING PLASTIC BUMPERS

Hairline cracks in plastic bumpers will usually disappear during the spraying process. If you have serious bumper damage (say, from a car park incident) use Isopon's Bumper Fill to produce a strong, but flexible result. The technique is the same as that used for filling dents in the bodywork as described

in Chapter 9. Having filled a bad crack or dent, you can paint the bumper as described earlier.

❑ HINTS AND TIPS

• The procedure described here refers to bumpers but, of course, it applies to all items of similar construction, such as wheelarch extensions.

• If you can, remove the bumper (or other trim item) before you spray; it's easier and there's less likelihood of areas being missed.

• Cleanliness is the key to a good finish. Get the workpiece scrupulously clean before giving it a final wipe over with thinners.

• Whenever spraying, work in a well-ventilated area, wear gloves when dealing with paint and thinners, etc., and take

Spray around 8 inches away from the bumper in thin coats.

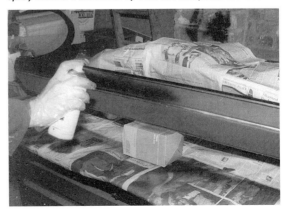

Now, doesn't that look better?

care to mask-off properly to prevent your workshop taking on a different hue.
  • If you get a blocked nozzle on an aerosol can, soak it in thinners (obeying the safety instructions). It may clear it.

WHEEL CARE
HOW TO KEEP WHEELS CLEAN, FIT WHEEL TRIMS OR RE-PAINT

❏ SAFETY
Please refer to Chapter 1 - working around your car whilst it has one or more wheels off the ground is potentially very dangerous.

Whenever you are spraying and/or using potentially harmful substances (thinners, paint, etc.) always work in a well-ventilated area. Do not spend long periods of time in the presence of harmful vapours - take a break and get some fresh air.

Asbestos: though many companies now produce asbestos-free brake pads, there are still plenty of pads which contain this dangerous substance. Take extreme care when dealing with brake dust - it's far from healthy to breathe it in. Use water to settle the dust, wear a mask and work in a well-ventilated area.

❏ FITTING WHEEL CLEAN DISCS
As shown in the valeting section, brake dust is evil stuff in more ways than one. The black dust sprays everywhere, notably onto your nice clean wheels, and is hard work to remove, particularly when it's been mixed with a little rain water. Fitting Wheel Clean Discs is one way to drastically reduce the amount of dust getting onto your wheels. Sold in pairs, they are suitable for applications up to 130mm PCD (pitch circle diamter), 3, 4 and 5 stud wheels. Effectively, they are flexible rubber 'shields' which fit inside the wheel and prevent brake dust blowing through onto the outside of the wheel.

Understandably, you might be cautious about this product - 'do the brakes overheat?' is the obvious query. The Wheel Clean Discs are fully approved by the German TUV organisation and its standards are extremely high. According to the test requirements, the product must not cause brake fade, over-heating of the hubs and brakes under extreme conditions or fouling of braking and/or suspension parts.

With the wheel removed from the car, the Wheel Clean Disc should be placed inside it and the holes centralised. The rubber 'skirt' should be an easy fit - if not it will have to be trimmed to size. Ordinary scissors can be used here and the job is made easier because a number of concentric circles are marked in the moulding. If your wheel is clean enough, the manufacturer suggests glueing the rubber edge of the trim to the inside of the wheel.

❏ FITTING WHEEL TRIMS
If you've cleaned your wheels and they still look awful, thanks to a combination of rust and old age, the easiest solution is to cover them up by fitting a set of wheel trims.

This Wheel Clean Disc is clearly too big for the wheel. It can easily be trimmed to size ...

... following the circles marked in the moulding. The edge can be glued to the inner wheel if required.

Top: Though clean, this little Pug was looking dowdy because of its wheels.

Middle: These Hella trims were chosen to suit the car's character. Extremely strong 'springs' give a firm friction fit. Ensure the valve is still accessible.

Below: Just ten minutes' work has improved the car's appearance no end and wheel cleaning is now much simpler.

(However, before fitting your trims it's a good idea to sand off the major rust areas and apply some rust preventative.)

Many manufacturers claim that their trims improve a car's aerodynamics, reduce its drag coefficient (cd) and therefore reduce petrol consumption. That's as may be; most owners simply fit them for their cosmetic appearance.

Though there are individual differences, most types of wheel trim fit by friction. It is vitally important the fit is perfect; losing a trim whilst you are travelling may be only an

inconvenience to you (albeit a costly one if you have to buy a complete set) but it could be very dangerous to other road users and/or pedestrians. It pays to check your car's trims on (at least) a weekly basis.

❏ SPRAYING STEEL WHEELS

A more permanent solution to the problem of unsightly rusty wheels is to respray them. Silver is the standard steel wheel colour, though other colours are available for those who want to customise their car a little. Many manufacturers produce aerosol spray paints specifically for wheels, the paint being tougher than normal.

Wheels can be painted while on the car but it's hard work and not recommended - you're unlikely to make a really good job of it and will run the risk of over-spraying onto the bodywork.

Start by removing all the dirt and grease from the wheels. De-rust them using a suitable sandpaper and wire brush and then apply an anti-rust solution: most have to be left overnight before they can be painted over.

When it comes to spraying remove the wheels and place newspaper over the wheel (broadsheets are best because you can cover the whole wheel in one go). Use a sharp knife to cut it to the shape of the rim - take the usual safety precautions when dealing with knives; always cut away from you and make sure you don't actually cut the tyre. Use masking tape to retain the paper where you want it. An alternative method is to cover the tyre wall with a coating of washing-up liquid. This means that the overspray can be washed off when the wheel is dry. Personally, as the latter offers the chance to damage the newly-painted rim, I'd take the first option.

All DIY aerosol sprays require some vig-

Top left: Clean the wheel and use a wire brush and sandpaper to prepare the surface for painting.

Middle left: Apply an anti-rust agent, otherwise you may soon be repeating this operation!

Bottom left: Use a sharp knife to cut the newspaper to the shape of the rim.

Top right: Spray evenly in a series of light coats. Remove masking tape when dry.

Right The finished job - just like new!

orous shaking before use, especially metallics. Don't stint at this point, eager though you may be to see some reward for your hard work thus far. Starting before the spray has fully mixed could undo everything. Shake for twice as long if you are working in cold weather.

Apply the usual spraying rules - spray from side to side in an even pattern and rely on a number of thin coats rather than trying to cover everything in one go.

When you've finished, check that no part of the wheel has been missed (especially around the valve stem) and let the paint dry thoroughly before removing the masking tape and newspaper. After this you'll probably want to return to the start of this section to seriously consider fitting Wheel Clean discs!

❏ TORQUE TALK

Once you've removed a wheel, make sure that you torque the wheel bolts to the correct tightness (see maker's handbook) when you replace it. Over-tightening not only runs the risk of damage to both wheel and bolt, it may also lead to embarrassing difficulties should you need to remove the wheel in the event of a puncture. It's a good idea to check after seven days or so that the bolts have not worked loose.

USING GLASSFIBRE & BODY FILLER

TECHNIQUES FOR FILLING DENTS AND BRIDGING HOLES

❏ SAFETY

SKIN IRRITATION & GLOVES

Glass fibre is well-known for causing skin irritation so it's important to always wear gloves when handling glass fibre matting.

Isopon provide a pair of plastic gloves with each Fastglas kit, but they are also available separately and will often come in useful when working on your car. Alternatively, many petrol stations provide them for customers' use when filling up with fuel. Rather than popping a used glove in the bin, pop it in your car's glovebox for re-use: waste not, want not!

Body fillers, too, are hardly kind to the skin. They contain powerful chemicals (not least the hardener) and once the stuff sets on your skin it's hard work to remove. Again, it's advisable to wear gloves of some description when working with filler.

FILLING

Using body filler usually requires that you sand down the paintwork and/or the filler itself. It's a wise move to use a mask (available at most DIY stores) to avoid inhaling the paint/filler dust.

PAINT

When using aerosol paints and/or thinners etc., always work in a well-ventilated area. Wear a mask if necessary and don't work for long periods without a break. Use plastic gloves to keep the paint and solvents off your skin.

❏ STRUCTURAL INTREGRITY

You can only patch and fill in areas which are not likely to affect the structural integrity and/or safety of the vehicle. This means definitely **NOT** on vehicle chassis or crossmembers, seat belt mounting points or sills, for example. In addition, the British MoT test states that glass fibre/filler must not be used within 30cm of certain load bearing items, such as suspension mountings. If you are in any doubt, check first,

before you start work.

❏ BODYWORK

The condition of the bodywork of a vehicle became part of the British MoT test in 1993. The intention is that your car should not pose a danger to other road users - on the carriageway or the pavement. Though some bodywork damage/corrosion is clearly dangerous, there are plenty of cases which fall into a grey area. However, as long as the area of damage (for example, a hole in the front wing), doesn't come under the heading of structural rigidity, then the DIY enthusiast can save time, money and a possible MoT failure by using the techniques described here. (Full details of MoT requirements are given in another Veloce book, *Pass the MoT*.

USING BODY FILLER TO REPAIR A DENT

In this section we deal with two different bodywork problems. The first is a dent in the rear nearside three-quarter panel of a Peugeot 205, the sort of thing that can easily happen in a car park any day of the week. The photographs on pages 35 and 36 (and the work!) were provided by Holt Lloyd Ltd., no strangers to the world of DIY bodywork repair.

Because the metal was barely penetrated, there was no need to reinforce the small holes before starting work. The first requirement was to create a 'valley' for the filler to sit in which is done by hammering a 'V' shape around the injured area. Then, the whole area has to be sanded down - start by using a fairly harsh grade paper, say, 120 grit, and progress to a finer grade (400/600) wet and dry. Where, as in this case, the damaged area meets good paintwork, the edge of the paintwork has to be 'feathered' in order to make the transition as easy as possible. Don't sandpaper with your fingers - wrap the paper around a block of wood or sponge. For larger areas, you can use a sander/grinder or electric drill with sander attachment.

Even though your car may have bared its metal for only a few hours, this is long enough for corrosion to get a hold. It's important to apply an anti-rusting agent before the paint.

FILLING THE HOLE

Most fillers require mixing with a hardener - follow the instructions and resist the temptation to mix too much. It goes off quicker than you'd think and it's not hard to mix up some more if you run out. Apply the filler using the plastic spreader supplied. If you're filling a deep hole, apply in thin layers, allowing each to dry before putting on the next. The objective is to get the filler about a paint layer thickness proud of the surrounding bodywork.

Where you're filling a complex body contour, an adjustable Surform plane or dreadnought file will help. If the panel is more or less flat, it's back to the sandpaper block again - coarse grade to start with, ending with a fine wet and dry paper.

Painting of this panel is shown and described in Chapter 10.

❏ GLASS FIBRE OR ALUMINIUM MESH

If you are repairing a hole (rather than a dent), you may get away with using just body filler. But if the hole is large enough, filler on its own won't do the job, so you'll need to patch the hole beforehand. The choice is whether to use glass fibre sheet or aluminium mesh. Which you choose will depend on personal preference and the position of the hole; as glass fibre matting has to be thoroughly wetted with resin/hardener, it is harder to use on very large holes and/or holes in vertical surfaces (for example, a door). Conversely, it is very easy to make it take almost any shape you want.

BRIDGING THE GAP

The accompanying pictures show the repair of a hole in a spare wheel wel; the hole was not an MoT failure point, which means that it did not have to be welded. The hole was large enough to require a 'bridge' - in this case glass fibre was chosen because it was a horizontal hole and it would be easy to blend the material to the circular shape required.

Having discovered an area of rotten

A wire brush in the electric drill was used to get rid of corrosion in the spare wheel well, then anti-rust agent applied to prevent a recurrence.

The sheet of glass fibre supplied in this Fastglas kit can be cut to size using scissors. Note the use of plastic gloves.

Having made sure that the patch is the right size, the resin was poured and then hardener mixed in.

Typical minor body damage like this is easily repairable on a diy basis.

A 'V' shape has to be made to form a valley for the filler.

Use progressively finer sandpapers and 'feather' into the edges of the good paint - note the use of a block.

An anti-rust agent is an essential part of the repair - otherwise you'll soon be repeating the operation!

metal like this, it's important that the true extent of the corrosion is ascertained (it can often spread under the paintwork much further than you might expect) and then to prevent it spreading further. If you can, use a power sander (or grinder with a sanding disc) to remove the surface rust. In this case, the contours of the body panel meant it was preferable to use a wire brush attachment in a powerful mains-powered drill (a cordless would not have enough

power for this kind of job).

Having got down to bare metal, the next step was to treat it to prevent further rusting. An anti-rust agent was applied to all the areas - the manufacturers claim that there is no need to remove all the rust, as it acts on it chemically. However, in cases like this, it is important to make sure that the rust is only on the surface and that there are no more holes waiting to pop through at any time; the corrosive tentacles of rust

Mix only as much filler paste as you can use quickly, following the maker's instructions.

Use a flexible spreader to apply the filler - build it up in thin layers rather than one large blob.

Then it's back to the sanding again - the use of a block prevents the filler taking on the 'shape' of your fingers.

penetrate far deeper than the area obviously affected.

Because of the agent's powerful nature, it's important to wear gloves. A little should be poured into a separate container (we used an old aerosol spray can lid) and applied direct. Once the dirty brush has been dipped in the liquid, it is effectively contaminated and whatever remains should not be returned to the original bottle. While we were in the area, we de-

rusted and treated several other areas of surface rust.

GLASS FIBRE

Unless you're going into glass fibre usage in a big way, the best method of fixing a hole is to buy a kit. The Fastglas product contains plastic gloves, a resin mixing cup and a wooden stirrer, together with differing quantities of glass fibre mat, resin and hardener.

Note at this point that gloves should be

worn. I can't emphasise enough just how irritating this stuff is if it gets on your skin.

You'll need to cut the glass fibre mat to size. With some jobs you'll have to take the mat to the work area, but here it was simple to measure how much matting was required and cut the piece to size. Glass fibre sheet is soft and flexible like cloth and can easily be cut to any shape required using ordinary household scissors. It's a wise move to take the cut piece to the area to be repaired and offer it up, just to ensure it's spot-on.

The information given in this section has drawn heavily on expertise provided by W. David & Sons, famous for the Isopon range of glass fibre and fillers for automotive repair.

MIXING AND APPLYING THE RESIN

The next job is to mix the resin and hardener. This is in the ratio of 20/30ml resin to 3/4cm of hardener. This does not call for too much accuracy and the ambient temperature will probably account for a greater difference in hardening times than the odd centimetre of hardener. It has to be mixed thoroughly using the wooden stirrer and, at this point, there is around 20 minutes available before it starts to go 'off'. Like filler, mix too little rather than too much to avoid wastage.

We took resin and mat to the repair area and, before the mat was applied, dabbed some resin around the edges of the hole. This acted like a glue and helped secure the mat in place while further resin was applied and stippled vigorously; it's important that every strand of glass fibre is covered.

The easy-going nature of glass fibre changes once it has been wetted with resin which has been activated by hardener; it forms a tough, glass fibre reinforced plastic which will permanently retain the shape in which it sets and will bond to most

materials. These properties make it ideal for car body repair work and, indeed, for car body customisation.

In ideal (*i.e.*, warm) conditions, it would take around 20 minutes for the patch to become touch-dry and quite hard. The cooler it is, the longer it will take to set. It is possible to speed up the drying time by using a hair dryer or even a fan heater, but care has to be taken - do not use either in poorly ventilated areas and take great care that the apparatus cannot cause a fire.

If a particularly strong patch is required, add further layers of glass fibre as necessary once the original(s) has dried.

When the resin has done its job, the glass fibre can be 'worked' almost like metal

The Isopon P40 was mixed as directed and then applied to the underside of the hole.

though, for the most part, with greater ease. It can be sanded where required, though in this case its position out of the way in the spare wheel well meant it was not necessary to make too much effort in that direction. (If you do sand glass fibre, you must wear a mask to avoid inhaling the dangerous particles.)

THE OTHER SIDE OF THE HOLE
At this stage the hole appears to have gone. Underneath, however, is an unsightly mess which requires filling.

Isopon produce two glass fibre reinforced fillers - P40 is used for bridging larger holes and where a final, mirror smooth finish is not critical; where it is, P38 should be used. The former was used here, mixing it with hardener on the lid of an old marga-

rine tub - keen DIY-ers will know the wisdom of never throwing anything away! It was applied to the damaged area using the plastic spreader. In this case, only a reasonably smooth line was required, though if it were being used on more visible bodywork it would be necessary to go through the sanding routine described earlier.

CLEANING UP
Only cellulose thinners or acetone will clean resin covered tools or brushes which have been used with Hammerite. Neither substance is pleasant to work with so take note of the safety warning at the start of this Chapter.

❏ USING GLASS FIBRE - HINTS & TIPS
• Always wear gloves of some description when dealing with glass fibre, its resin, body filler or chemical rust neutralisers.

• Do not mix more resin than you can apply in 5 minutes - it is quick setting. More resin can be mixed quite easily.

• When sticking glass fibre to any material, apply the same basic rules as you would when glueing - the surface should be clean and grease-free and, ideally, roughened slightly to offer a 'key'.

• Any repair area can be strengthened considerably by applying a second layer of glass fibre once the original layer has stared to harden.

• Any surplus can be neatly trimmed by using a sharp craft knife once the resin has started to set.

❏ USING FILLER - HINTS AND TIPS
HARDENING TIMES
• Using more hardener/hotter temperature will make the paste harden more quickly (and the reverse is true).

• Mix up a small amount just to see how long it does take to go 'off' in the particular conditions you're working in.

• The paste is usable until it begins to gel or stiffen, which is usually around 5-10 minutes.

• A clean polythene sheet or piece of cardboard is ideal for mixing on.

• The paste/hardener is thoroughly mixed when there are no traces of the (different coloured) hardener showing in the mixture.

PAINTING
PAINTING TECHNIQUES AND THE USE OF AEROSOLS

❏ MASKING-OFF

Masking tape comes in various widths - if you've a roll each of half inch and one inch in your tool box you'll always have a use for them. Whenever you are working on or around your car's bodywork it pays to make sure that you cannot damage or over-spray adjacent paintwork or glass. If you are sanding down a small area (as in

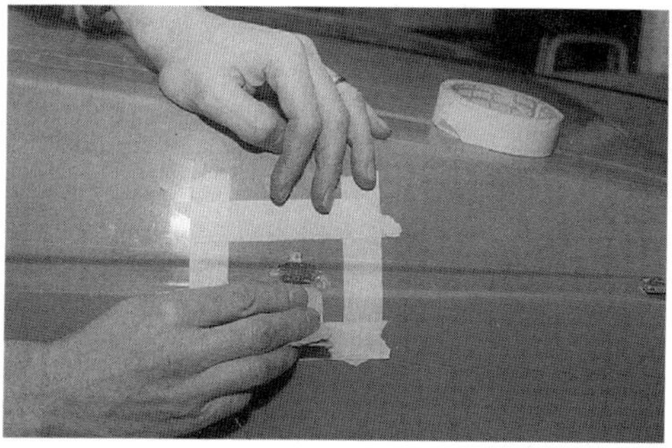

If you're working on a small area of bodywork, mask-off like this to prevent damaging the surrounding paint.

the case of a stone chip) use masking tape to square off the area you're working in so that you don't accidentally sand the good paint.

If you're spraying, the masking-off procedure has to be much more thorough. Again, masking tape is used to contain the paint in the area required, but it has to be used with sheets of newspaper so that the entire area is protected. For fiddly items (wing mirrors, etc.,) masking tape can be wound around to 'mummify' the object in question. Even if you've removed the item to be sprayed (a bumper, for example) you still have to be careful that you don't also accidentally spray everything in your workshop!

❏ PROTECTING RUBBER SEALING STRIPS

Over-spray on rubber sealing strips (around

windows and doors, etc.,) is a sure sign that someone has been over-enthusiastic with the spray can! To make sure this isn't you take a length of string and press it under the edge of the seal so that it is raised very slightly and apply the masking tape to the seal as usual. Because the seal is raised, the paint will go under it and not on the rubber - a perfect finish.

❏ GETTING THE RIGHT COLOUR

Before you rush down to the shop to buy your paint, it's important to note you should use paint of the right colour - exactly the right colour. Ford, for example, have used dozens of different reds over the years. Most cars have a sticker (usually in the boot or hatch) giving details of the precise colour reference. If you can't find yours, contact your local dealer who should be able to help. If nothing else, it's often possible to work out the name of, say, a particular shade of red, by working through the model years (colours, like clothes, tend to come in and out of fashion and are used for some seasons and not for others).

If you are still unsure, or if the car has been resprayed a non-standard colour, try your local paint supplier for help in identification.

❏ STONE CHIPS

Touching-up small, stone-chipped areas is a chore but one well worth completing on a regular basis. Not only will your car look better, you will also defer the onset of rust; a small spot of bare metal will soon become a tiny circle of rust, anxious to grow and develop into a fully-fledged hole.

You can buy touch-up kits from the manufacturer or purchase a proprietary version of the type shown here. Companies such as Auto-K produce a range of aerosol 'packages' which, as well as providing the aerosol paint, include in the transparent lid a couple of small sheets of

These touch-up sprays are available in most standard colours ..

... and include a small brush, sandpaper and a sachet of body stopper.

sandpaper, a small pack of stopper, an applicator and a tiny brush.

For a typical stone chip (the bonnet is literally in the firing line for this kind of damage), clean the area using white spirit to get rid of any grease and sandpaper to roughen the bared metal.

400 grade wet and dry is about right, as you'll not be able to avoid the surrounding paintwork; this grade will roughen the paint sufficiently enough to offer a key to the new paint but not to gouge holes in it. It's advisable to apply

Use the sandpaper to remove any surface corrosion. If necessary, use the stopper to build up the level of the hole.

a spot of anti-rust agent to the mark, otherwise you could end up with a corrosion problem.

Stopper (or cellulose putty) is used to build up the level to equal the surrounding paint - you may or may not find this necessary. Once this has set, carefully sand it to a smooth finish. It's a good idea to mask-off the area with masking tape (as described earlier), so you don't accidentally sand down the good adjacent paintwork.

The spray from the nozzle of the aerosol is far too wide for such a small area. However, you can 'cheat' by spraying a small amount of paint into the aerosol cap and then using a tiny touch-up brush to apply it to the area in question.

❑ USING TOUCH-UP ADHESIVE STRIPS

A variation on the touch-up theme is the self-adhesive paint strip - both Holts and

It's a good idea to apply a drop of anti-rust agent to stone chips before painting.

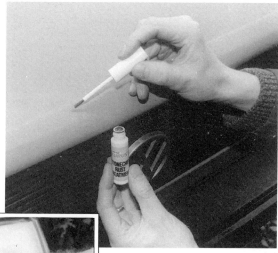

Areas like this are really too small to spray, but you can 'cheat' by spraying the paint into the lid and ...

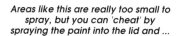

able to hear the metal ball rattling as you shake it. A constant two minutes is a minimum, much longer if the ambient temperature is low. Agitate occasionally in-between spraying.

• Hold the spray can around 8 inches away from the item and move the can parallel to the workpiece.

• Don't try and cover every-

... painting it into the chip using a small brush.

Auto-K offer variants. It's a cleaner, simpler way to apply paint to small areas of your car and is effectively a sheet of self-adhesive strips of paint, the same colour as your car. The strips are 'scored' into various sizes; after preparing the area as already described, choose the right size strip for your application, peel it off and place it onto the affected area. As simple as that!

❑ BASIC AEROSOL SPRAYING TECHNIQUES

• Spend a long time agitating the aerosol thoroughly; you will be

Top: An alternative to conventional paint touch-ups is this self-adhesive 'paint in a strip'.

Middle: You just peel off a strip of the right size to suit the damaged area and ...

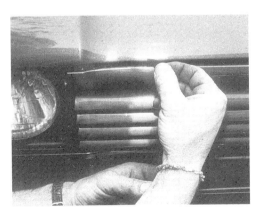

Bottom: ... place it on the bodywork. Simple as that!

and stop just after you've reached the end: sometimes the starting and stopping process results in a 'spluttering' from the can, which will mess up all your hard work.

• If you don't keep the can parallel with the workpiece, an uneven finish - and, possibly, runs in the paint in the centre section which receives more paint than the sides - will result.

• When spraying a horizontal surface, such as the bonnet of your car, tip the can at an angle of 45 degrees. Go any closer to the 90 degree right-angle and you risk the nozzle spluttering and/or dripping drops of paint onto your work.

• Applying paint from an aerosol onto a small area can be achieved by spraying a little into the lid and using a small modellers' brush.

• When you've finished spraying with aerosol, invert the can and spray at some of the masking newspaper you've been using. That way, the nozzle will not clog with paint.

❏ METALLIC PAINTWORK

Spraying metallic paintwork is a work of art and a true test of patience. Much will depend on the angle the spray can is held at and it is advisable to spend a lot of time trying out various angles and techniques on a piece of scrap metal before applying the paint to your car. When it comes to cutting and waxing, don't forget that metallic paint is generally 'softer' and a specific wax polish should be used.

❏ PAINTING A DAMAGED AND REPAIRED BODY PANEL

In Chapter 9, we saw how Holt Lloyd repaired a dent in the rear of a typical car. The photos here show how the job was completed. (The same principles apply to all aerosol spraying jobs, even if

thing in one go - build up the colour in a number of light passes. Start spraying slightly to one side of the area you want to cover

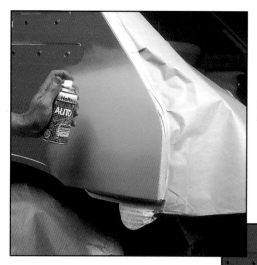

Having sanded down the body filler, aerosol primer was applied.

This was then sanded down again, using a fine grade wet and dry paper for best results.

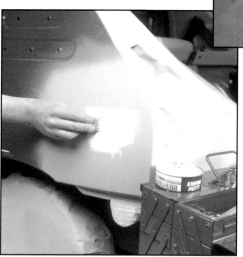

Knifing putty was applied to fill in any tiny inconsistencies. When dry, this was sanded again and a further coat of primer applied.

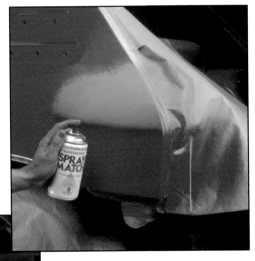

When the finish was perfectly smooth, the
aerosol top coat was applied.

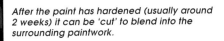

After the paint has hardened (usually around
2 weeks) it can be 'cut' to blend into the
surrounding paintwork.

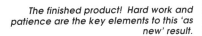

The finished product! Hard work and
patience are the key elements to this 'as
new' result.

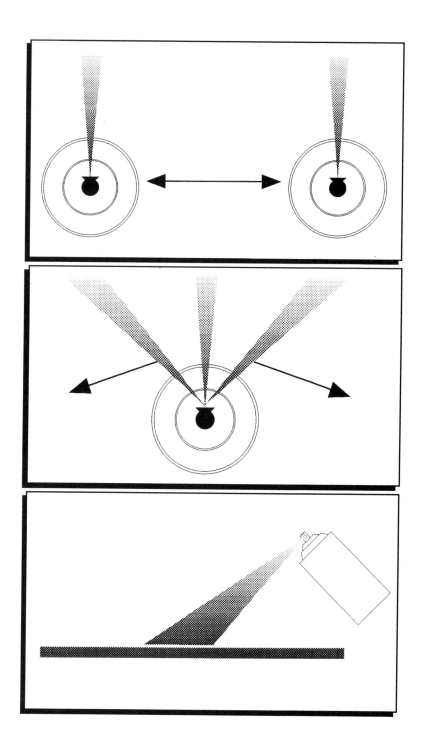

Top left: CORRECT - Move the can parallel to the workpiece.

Middle left: INCORRECT - Allowing the can to swivel with your wrist movement will result in an uneven finish.

Bottom left: When spraying horizontal surfaces, use the same techniques, but spray at an angle of 45 degrees.

you haven't been filling beforehand.)

Having sanded the filler as flush as possible, primer has to be applied. Because it's exterior bodywork, an aerosol spray primer was preferred (to the brush-on versions) in order to give a better finish. Around 1 inch of the surrounding 'good' paintwork should be overlapped with primer.

When the primer had dried, it was sanded again with fine (400 grade) wet and dry paper before knifing putty (or body stopper) was applied in the same way as the body filler. (If required, this can be watered down). The putty 'flowed' into the tiny cracks and, when dry, was sanded with fine wet and dry paper again and treated to a second coat of primer. At this point, the surface and primer should be ready for the final coat. If there are still imperfections the knifing putty/sanding and primer/sanding operations should be repeated until a really smooth finish is attained.

Body colour-matched paint was applied following the basic rules of aerosol spraying shown in the diagrams in this chapter.

❑ BLENDING IN AFTER AEROSOL SPRAYING

Unless you're working with a very new car, it's unlikely a newly-sprayed area will exactly match the existing paintwork. To help blend the two together let the new paint harden for two weeks and then use a cutting agent on the original paintwork around the new 'patch' and on the edges of the patch itself. Waxing the whole area should result in the new integrating seamlessly with the old. However, if the original paintwork has faded too badly, it may be necessary to paint a whole panel.

BODY PROTECTION
ACCESSORIES TO PROTECT YOUR CAR'S BODY

The need for rectification work on your car's exterior is the result of a lack of protection. Here are a few ideas on how you can protect your car against some of its more common assailants.

❏ MUD, GLORIOUS MUD
All the mud that collects along the bottom

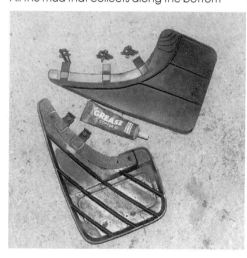

These mudflaps feature two different types of bolt-on clamps. Either is preferable to drilling holes in the wheelarch.

of your car encourages rust. You can reduce the amount of mud that sticks by fitting a set of mudflaps. Most are easy enough to fit, the methods generally being either a) drilling the edge of the wheelarch to attach by means of self-tapping screws or b) simple metal clips which clamp the mudflap to the wheelarch. The benefit of the latter means is that you don't have to drill a hole in the bodywork which, no matter how much you rustproof it, becomes another potential rust target. Most mudflaps are held in place by some kind of clamp secured by a 10mm bolt. At the top is a flap which clamps directly onto the edge of the wing. If you use this kind, it's important to apply a little rustproofing as well, because it's possible the clamps could damage the paintwork. The lower flap has a plastic 'lip' which folds over the edge of the wing and the metal clamp fits to this, preventing the possibility of damage.

Fitting flaps at the front will help protect the sills - a particularly vulnerable area and one which can be a source of an MoT failure certificate. Fit flaps at the rear to prevent rot starting around the

Most clamps lock using 10mm bolts. Use a socket if you can or ring spanner if space is tight.

The finished job improves appearance and keeps mud at bay.

rear wheelarches and valence.

❏ DOOR EDGE PROTECTORS

One of the most common recipients of touch-up paint is the area along the edge of the door. Having been scratched and marked by fingernails and keys, it also suffers from parking damage. It's a good idea to fit a set (two or four, depending on your car) of door edge protectors.

These come either with a peel-off adhesive backing or clip over the edge of the door. Don't have any doubts as to the potency of the glue used - it's strong stuff, which means that you must take great care to get the position right first time. Don't forget that any surface to be glued should be clean and grease-free. If you're using the clip-on variety, it's a good idea to use a spot of glue to ensure they stay put. Some makes feature a rear-facing red reflector for the owner's safety and a maker's motif in the centre for the owner's vanity!

❏ HEADLAMP PROTECTION

At the front of the car a broken headlamp is a pain in the pocket and possibly an MoT failure point. One of the best ways to avoid this is to place a protective transparent plastic cover over them. Signam make a variety of 'sized' covers (Smoothy Lightguards), whereas Metro supply the sheets of lined plastic ready to be cut to whatever size and shape required. If you've got circular headlamps, the simplest way

Fit protectors like these to safeguard your door edges ...

... just peel off the backing and stick in place. These have a built-in red reflector.

Five pounds' worth of protection; a hundred pounds' worth of headlamp - no contest!

The exact shape of the headlamp has to be transferred to the plastic sheeting.

to get a perfect circle is to use a school compass with the chinagraph pencil supplied with the kit. Male/female velcro tabs are supplied to be stuck on the headlamp and at matching points on the cover which is held securely in place but is easy to remove also.

Not only can covers be used for the vehicle's standard fixed lighting, but also for auxiliary lights, particularly fog lamps, which tend to be mounted nearer the ground and even more in the 'danger zone'.

❏ BUMPER TRIM STRIPS

It sounds a contradiction in terms, but you can save yourself some grief by protecting your bumpers. Obviously, a really hard knock is going to

The bumper trim strip comes in rolls. There's a sister product which fits to the wheelarches.

damage them come what may, but supermarket scrapes can be minimised by fitting a bumper trim strip (which some models feature as standard). The type shown here is available in various colours, though red on a black bumper is a popular choice. The strip simply sticks to the bumper, so make sure the bumper's spotlessly clean. Give the area in question a final wipe-over with white spirit or thinners (try this first on a hidden part of the bumper to ensure no adverse reaction). On most bumpers there is a natural line to follow which makes fitting the trim strip much easier. Even so, take your time and make regular checks that it is absolutely straight. A slight error at one end will become huge at the other; stand back every foot or so and check it out. Where there is no obvious line to follow, try

Unrolling and heating the roll aids fitting. The bumper must be free from dirt and grease.

the masking tape tip described under the next heading.

❏ BODY RUBBING STRIPS

Many cars come with these fitted as standard. In essence, they are just lumps of rubber stuck along the side of the car which act as a barrier against all those drivers who use their ears rather than their eyes when parking! It's usually possible to buy them as aftermarket kits and they are applied in much the same way as the bumper inserts. Again, it's important that the surface should be clean.

When you're sticking to bodywork, choose a warm day or, failing that, break out the hair dryer again and heat both the glued area on the body moulding and the bodywork itself. Be careful not to apply too much heat in a localised area on your paintwork, otherwise you'll end up with a heat blister!

If you've an existing body line to follow, getting the moulding straight is fairly easy. If you haven't (or want to position it elsewhere) then some preliminary work is called for. Measure the height required and mark the position with a piece of masking tape. Do this at points approx 12 inches apart down the length of the car; use the tape as markers for the position you want and remove it once you are satisfied with the position of the moulding.

It will look much neater if you trim the ends to match your bumper shape.

The trim just sticks into place. Take care to get it straight or it will look ridiculous.

DEALING WITH RUST
TECHNIQUES FOR RUST REMOVAL AND RUSTPROOFING

❏ SAFETY

Safety warnings relate mainly to the protection of your skin and your eyes when removing loose rust and/or paint. In addition, most anti-rust agents contain strong chemicals and gloves should be worn at all times when dealing with them. Should you splash any on your skin, apply copious amounts of water.

Apply the usual safety rules when working with electronic machinery, especially if you have a long extension lead which could easily be trapped or severed.

❏ INSIDE OUT

Rust is the car owner's worst enemy. It's powerful, silent and never takes a tea break! If you have a galvanised car, you're allowed a smug smile at this point, although even then rust problems can occur where a repair has not been carried out correctly. Fibreglass-bodied cars, too, have steel chassis members which are sadly susceptible to the old corrosion bug. Chapter 9 has some horrific examples of what rust can do when not checked.

The magnetic 'Spot Rot' device is one of the simplest ways to detect hidden rusty metal or filler.

There are many body sections on a car which are hollow and provide the perfect breeding place for rust, the most obvious being the sills. Moisture can sit inside and work away at the paint over a period of years. If you don't take adequate precautions, the first you know of it is when the outer

Trouble below - these rust bubbles are what you get when you don't rustproof on a regular basis.

paintwork starts to bubble. It's important to get some anti-rust agent into any such areas as soon as possible.

❏ SILLS AND CLOSED STRUCTURES

There are (or should be) a number of rubber drain plugs on your car - they are fitted to hollow sections where moisture can accumulate. These are there to let this moisture drain away, but this can't happen if you don't get around to removing them every now and then. Just as important is to remember to replace them when you've fin-

A mini-grinder/sander, like this B & D model, or an electric drill and wire brush are ideal for anti-rust work.

... enable you to get an extension pipe in from another angle.

ished - a plug which lets water out can just as easily let water in! These plugs can also act as ideal places to spray in Waxoyl, which is still one of the best ways to protect hard-to-get-at areas like sills. It is, by nature, a creeping substance, which enables it to cover large areas of metal, cutting off air supply and dispersing water. Once dry it forms a tough but flexible coating.

Waxoyl sell an air pressure spray gun with extensions to enable you to reach places you didn't even know were there. If you can't complete the job by using existing access holes, it's worth drilling one or two extra holes in order to get that metal-preserving fluid injected. Make sure you treat the edges of a newly-drilled hole with anti-rust agent, otherwise this exercise is self-defeating! You can buy rubber bungs at most DIY stores so that you can plug the new hole.

Waxoyl (and similar rust preventatives) work better when warm, which is one good reason for doing the job in the summer. (Another is that it's no fun crawling around under your car in the depths of winter!) If the temperature is on the low side, it's a good idea to stand the can in a bucket of warm water which will help it flow where it should. Alternatively, it can be mixed with white spirit.

❑ DOORS
The Waxoyl extension tube can be used again to spray the inside of the lower doors with rust-proofing fluid. It's important not to get it on the windows, so they need to be wound right up. After removing the door trim, peel back the plastic covering carefully - don't damage it as it is designed to

keep any damp out of the cabin. Rust in doors tends to occur mainly from halfway down, which is where you should concentrate your efforts. When finished, seal the plastic covering back into position. If it has split at any point, use electrician's tape to cover it. Make sure that door drain holes are kept clear.

❑ TAILGATE LID
Inside the tailgate is another place where rust can start and it should be treated like the doors, although there isn't usually a plastic cover to contend with.

Peel back or take off the interior trim and apply Waxoyl to the lower edges of the doors and window-winder mechanism - not the glass or radio speakers, though. (Courtesy Hammerite Products Ltd)

□ STICKY BUSINESS

Waxoyl won't usually harm electrics, rubber or plastic products (though it will make them very sticky) but you don't want to get it onto the glass or your hands; it won't harm you and it's non-poisonous, but you'll cover everything you touch with it and it's hard to get off. Use hand cleaner to remove it from glass surfaces and wear plastic gloves to keep your hands clean.

□ HINTS AND TIPS

• Rustproofers such as Waxoyl should not be applied directly to exhaust components, including baffle boxes and mani-

The area under the wheelarches takes a real pounding. De-rust and use Finnegan's Underbody Seal to protect.
(Courtesy Hammerite Products Ltd)

Use Underbody Seal and Waxoyl as appropriate on chassis/box sections and floor pan, both of which are MoT failure items. (Courtesy Hammerite Products Ltd)

folds.

• Though useful for protecting metal brake lines and junctions, Waxoyl should not be allowed to get onto braking friction components. When you are working in their vicinity, use plastic bags secured with

elastic bands to protect discs, calipers and drums.

• Don't be afraid to drill an extra hole or two in order to get Waxoyl into difficult-to-get-at box sections. It's better than having to repair major rust damage!

□ UNDERSEAL

For protecting exposed areas, such as under the wheelarches or floor pan, you need to use something like Finnegan's Underbody Seal. This sticky black substance also contains Waxoyl which helps it to stay flexible and gives it a tendency to 'creep' into small, awkward places. Be extremely wary of many conventional bitumen underseals which become brittle with age; the surface can crack and allow water to sit behind it, quietly rotting the bodywork.

Apply the underseal copiously to a clean, dry surface and, following the note below, it should be checked carefully each year to ensure that it is still in place and providing full protection. With the battering it takes, it may well need replacing.

□ AND THE REST

Where else to spray the rust-proofing fluid depends on your car - all models have their own individual rust traps which you should seek out with a vengeance. Get a good covering of Waxoyl wherever water could collect and start to eat into the bodywork.

□ FRAYING AT THE EDGES

Sills and wheelarches are constantly under attack from stones, which chip away the paint surface, revealing bare metal and allowing rust to start in earnest.

If this is your problem (as in the picture sequence shown here) then your first job is to remove any trim pieces. You'll probably find, as we did, that the concave rear of the trim piece has filled with dirt. This traps moisture and holds it against the paintwork, where it could well form a rust spot in time. We cleaned out dirt and applied a thick layer of Waxoyl to prevent a recurrence.

To get rid of the bubbling paintwork and thick rust to the point where you can see metal again, you can use an electric grinder/sander or, as we did, a wire brush

Fitting plastic wheelarch spats covers up rust-affected arches and protects against further damage. But before you fit them, that rust has to go. Note the use of newspaper to protect interior from the dust and debris.

Before tackling the sill, remove any trim pieces.

Clean dirt accumulations from the back of trim pieces which hold moisture against the metal. Spray with Waxoyl to prevent a recurrence.

With all the rotten paintwork removed, apply an anti-rust agent and allow time for it to work.

mounted in an electric drill. Take care to wear gloves and eye protection with all those flakes of paint and rotten metal flying around. As the doors had to be open to get to the metal at the top of the sill, we used masking tape and sheets of newspaper to prevent too much dust getting onto the upholstery.

Apply an anti-rust agent before putting on paint of any description. Take note of the individual instructions with regard to safety and the drying time required before top coats can be applied. Agents such as Loctite's Rust Remedy can be seen to be working within 15 minutes by the change of colour of the affected areas to a dark purple.

We were pleased to find that there were no holes in the sills, this area being an MoT failure point (and thus any holes would have to be welded rather than filled using glass fibre, etc.)

Any large holes in the wheelarches can be sorted as detailed in Chapter 9 by using filler and/or aluminium mesh/glass fibre. Small holes can be filled using body stopper.

❏ PRIME TIME

Effective though the rust treatment is, it's not wise to apply paint directly to bare metal. Our choice of primer was Finnegan's No 1 Rust Beater, which has heat-hardened glass flakes suspended in it for added protection against those troublesome stone chips.

If the job was to finish with an aerosol spray to match the body colour, the primer (available in aerosol format) could have been sprayed on. However, we had decided to fit plastic wheelarch extensions (which are available for a wide variety of

*Before final coats of paint are
applied, paint the wheelarch edges
and sill with primer.*

cars from a number of aftermarket specialists). Therefore, as the final finish was not so important the primer was painted on with a brush.

❏ APPLYING A PROTECTIVE PAINT FINISH

Once this had dried, we applied black Hammerite smooth finish around the wheelarches and along the sill. Again, and for the same reasons, it was acceptable to use a brush rather than aerosol spray. In

As we were fitting wheelarch extensions we finished off with a coating of black Hammerite.

and aluminium particles, which bind together to provide a barrier against moisture. The makers claim it can be applied directly onto rust, but you must make sure that any rust is only surface rust and has not penetrated the metal; the best way to do that is to carry out a vigorous wire brush routine as described earlier. Anyway, I'm a great believer in the 'belt, braces and then another belt' theory of rust prevention - you just can't have too much!

❏ FITTING WHEELARCH EXTENSIONS

Wheelarch extensions shown here are available for many makes and models and are a good way to cover up tatty wheelarches. More importantly, the MoT regulations regarding unsafe bodywork could well mean that wheelarches with protruding rusty edges are illegal.

It's no good just putting them over rust, of course, and there must be some good metal for the screws to 'bite' into, otherwise the extensions themselves could become a danger! The positions of the self-tapping screws are marked in the plastic and it's a fairly simple task to hold the extensions in place and drill the holes. It's a good idea to secure them to the wing by using a few strips of masking tape so that

addition, as the sills are subject to a fierce battering from the elements, stone chips and road dirt of all descriptions, it is important to ensure that the sills receive a really thick coating of Hammerite, something more easily achieved by hand brushing. It was necessary to use masking tape to prevent the paint going where it wasn't required, particularly on the top edge of the sill inside the car.

The reason for Hammerite's success lies in its composition: it contains high quality base resins, pigments, heat-hardened glass they can't slip at a crucial moment. Being lighter and more manoeuvrable, the cordless drill is a boon when doing jobs like this.

Before fixing the extensions in place, a coating of Waxoyl was brushed along the edge which was to be covered: it forms an extra barrier against moisture and road dirt that manages to get down behind the extensions - and it will, no matter how tight you screw them on!

Extensions have pre-drilled holes ready for the self-tapping screws.

to be stirred well before and during the painting operation. It should dry in around half-an-hour, though in cooler weather it will take longer.

As ever, it's important not to breathe in paint fumes; work outside or in a well-ventilated area.

❑ UNDER THE BONNET
Waxoyl can be used to great effect in the engine bay. The battery mounting tray is often an area of rust as the battery acid eats through first the paint and then the metal. Treat with bicarbonate of soda to neutralise any acid before applying Waxoyl. The inner wings and tops of suspension mountings will benefit from protection and spraying electrical components (such as the distributor and spark plugs) will make them

We used masking tape to hold them in place whilst the holes were marked and ...

... drilled. A cordless drill is ideal for this kind of job.

❑ WHEEL DEALING
It's not just on the outside where a protective paint finish is required. As seen in Chapter 9, areas such as the spare wheel well are a natural rusting place.

We treated the rusty areas with anti-rust agent and roughed the area over a little with sandpaper. As the main area at risk was the bottom of the wheel well, we masked off a neat circle on the bottom half. We decided to apply Hammerite hammer finish which, like all such protective paints, has

To prevent further rust problems with our rogue spare wheel well (see Chapter 9), we masked off the lower section ...

... and applied a coating of Hammerite. Note the stirrer in situ - it has to be stirred at regular intervals. Again, plastic gloves were worn.

waterproof and aid starting in damp and cold conditions.

❏ AN ANNUAL EVENT

It's important to realise that no matter how much attention you pay to rust-proofing this year, next year, you will have to repeat the procedure. Anything can happen in a year; for example, you may have missed a youthful patch of surface rust which could have spent the last 365 days maturing into a fully-fledged hole!

INTERIOR VALETING
CLEANING TECHNIQUES AND USEFUL ACCESSORIES

❏ TIDYING UP

Cleaning the interior of the car tends to be one of those jobs that gets left in favour of more 'important' matters. However, driving a dirty, untidy car can cost you money or even involve you in an accident! How? Anyone can tell you that a clean car (inside and out) is more saleable than a scruffy one and when dirt has been ingrained over a period of months (or even years) it's often impossible to remove a mark which could otherwise have been sorted. And many crashes have been caused by unidentified rolling objects finding their way under the driver's pedals ...

So, the first aspect of interior valeting is to tidy up. Remove the carpet mats (if fitted) and work your way through the car, emptying it as you go. It can be an unpleasant task (especially if you have children, who tend to leave used chewing gum in the most amazing places!) but console yourself with the thought that you might well find the odd pound coin or two.

❏ CREATING MORE STORAGE SPACE

If you've a tendency to be particularly untidy in car, or have an older car (they usually have much less storage space), there are ways to make life easier. A centre console will provide space for

Fitting a Quickfit 70 centre console is easy - just three holes to drill and three self-tapping screws to hold it in place.

This model has space for 6 cassettes (no more searching under the seats) and an aperture for a head unit or, as in this case, a Fischer C-Box CD carrier.

storing bits and pieces and/or cassettes/CDs, etc. Cassettes especially do not benefit by being stored under a dirty seat!

Another way to gain interior space is to fit door pockets. Autoplas is one of many companies to produce a range to suit most cars which simply screw into place on the door panel. You will have to ensure they do not foul on the door handle or window winder and also that they do not mask a speaker grille.

Metro Products produce the Car Tidy and the Boot Tidy - self-explanatory names for items which fit onto a seat back or boot respectively and provide a number of storage pockets. Worth considering if you're habitually untidy.

❏ CLEANING

When you are cleaning your car's headlining, carpet or seats, there are various proprietary products on the market you can use. Whichever you choose, try a small, out-of-the-way piece of the relevant trim first, to make sure that it is colour fast and there are no adverse reactions - you can't be too careful. For preference, work outside with the doors open to aid the drying procedure and prevent condensation problems.

Don't forget that in-

Right: The Metro Products Car Tidy is a good idea for in-car storage.

Below: The Boot Tidy does the same job in the luggage area.

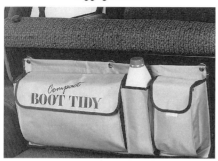

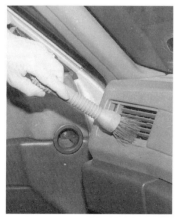

Get dust from those awkward places by using a wheel cleaning brush or a (clean) paintbrush.

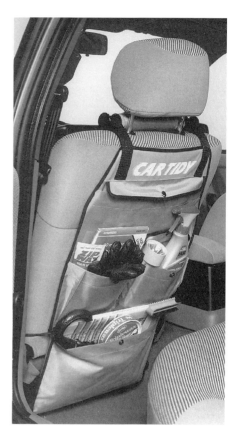

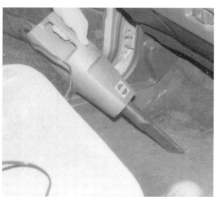

A high-power car vacuum will get rid of the dirt and grit from your carpet.

terior cleaning also means the boot or hatch - a sadly neglected area of most cars.

❏ VACUUMING

In general, you should start at the top and work down. Conversely, start by vacuuming the carpet, as the dust created will fly everywhere, defeating the object of cleaning anything else first. Like household carpets, wear comes largely from grit in the pile rubbing against it, so it's a good idea to brush or vacuum regularly. If you can kidnap the household wet 'n dry vac for half-an-hour that will do nicely, but remember the safety rules, especially those concerning water (*i.e.* rain) and electricity. A simpler way is to use a 12v cleaner powered by the car's electrical system - most run off a cigar lighter, though it's a simple task to remove such a plug and fit a couple of crocodile clips to enable it to run directly from the battery. When you're using a car-powered cleaner, bear in mind that they can take a lot out of the battery, especially if it's not fully charged to start with.

Caked-on mud is likely to be common-place, so make sure you get it all off - use a stiff brush in conjunction with the power cleaner where it's really stubborn.

Having vacuumed the carpet thoroughly, you'll probably have discovered one or two marks you didn't know were there. However, carpet shampooing comes later - we're now going back to the top.

❑ HEADLINING NEWS

In relatively new cars, dirt on the headlining should be fairly easy to remove, but not so easy as the years go by. Start by trying a purpose-made car upholstery cleaner, such as Turtle Wax Renew. Spray it on and wait the time specified on the label. If the stain is really stubborn, it may be necessary to work the cleaner into it with a stiff brush - an old toothbrush is often ideal.

As they get older, car headlinings become ever more problematical, largely because they tend to be ignored for so many years. In addition, if one or more of the regular occupants smokes, there will be no small amount of discolouring.

If none of the standard trim cleaners work, a household cleaner may be stronger and do the trick (but remember the caveat about trying it on a small piece first).

If you can't get the headlining clean, there are only two options, the first of which is to paint it. This is not quite as drastic as it sounds, as there are a number of vinyl trim paints which can be sprayed or brushed on. Ensure adjacent areas are well masked-off, especially when spraying.

And the second option? Replace the headlining, an expensive and tricky operation, even for a professional.

Turtle Wax Carisma is a multi-purpose cleaner suitable for most areas of interior trim. Spray on and wipe off. Don't get it on glass or safety items such as the pedal rubbers.

❑ VINYL TRIM

The interior trim in most cars will either be card-backed, vinyl or stipple-finish plastic. Both types of panels can be cleaned of excess dirt and dust by using a cloth soaked in warm water. For a clean sheen, use a cleaner such as Turtle Wax Carisma or Comma's Cockpit spray. If you use a cleaner of the spray-on type, it's sometimes best to spray directly into your cloth to avoid the possibility of getting spray on your seats or the interior glass.

❑ WOODEN TRIM

Those with 'prestige' cars (or prestige models of standard cars) may have a spot of wood around somewhere. Most standard interior trim cleaners will clean/polish wood as well. Again, don't get polish of this nature on glass or safety items such as the steering wheel or pedal rubbers.

❑ GLASS

Though the outside of the car's glass gets a clean every time you wash the car, many owners don't bother at all with the inside. If you're one of these, there's a big surprise waiting for you when you see just how much sticky dirt comes off the average interior glass surface - particularly if the car is used by smokers. As with the outside, it's important to use a non-smear cleaner so that your view is not obscured in any way - use something of the nature of Turtle Wax glass cleaner with a lint-free cloth.

In the course of your glass-cleaning exercise, you might discover the cause of your non-functioning rear window demister - the usual case is that one of the elements has been damaged at some time. Use Comma's Electrocure, a 'liquid metal'

Don't forget the windows. Spray on the cleaner and wipe off. You'll probably be surprised at how much more light there now is in the car!

Use Comma's Electrocure to repair damaged heater elements in the rear screen.

painted onto the damaged area, to restore the vital contact. It's best to apply it in thin coats, allowing time to dry between each.

❏ SEATS

Most cars have either cloth-covered seats, of the 'tweed' finish variety or seats covered in a 'velour' finish. It's usually only 'upmarket' models that benefit from leather (or part leather) seats - unless you've fitted aftermarket seats, of course. If it doesn't look like rain, it's a good idea to remove the seats altogether - with improved access, you're likely to do a much better job.

Whichever kind of seat you have, the first task is to give them a once-over with a soft brush and/or vacuum. Make sure you get right down the back of the seats and down the sides where the tilt mechanisms are, which can often make a world of difference on its own. Where a seat is generally grubby but without any specific nasty staining, a proprietary upholstery

cleaner, such as Turtle Wax Renew, should bring out the original colour.

The usual method of use is to apply the cleaner - usually a foam - and leave it for a while (as specified on the label) before wiping over with a damp cloth. The cleaner works by 'lifting' the dirt out into the foam. If you're lucky, this will be the end of your seat-cleaning operations. All-too-often, however, it's the cue for some specialised stain removing, as you discover marks you didn't realise were there. (If you discover any actual damage to the seat refer to Chapter 13.) The stain-removing guide at the end of this section gives details of how to deal with the most common stains you're likely to encounter.

LEATHER SEATS
If you have leather seats (lucky you!), repeat the brushing/vacuuming operation, though with more care so that you don't scratch the leather. Use a soft cloth and warm water to wipe off any ingrained dirt - don't use harsh chemicals.

For leather seats, you need to turn to a specialist and the most famous of all when it comes to leather is Connolly's. They produce a cleaner for when the seats are really dirty and their CeeBee hide food will help keep the leather supple once clean.

THE COVER-UP
Fitting a set of seat covers is a way to prevent the original seat coverings fading. If nothing else, this will up the ante when it comes to selling your car. If you're too late, you can use them to cover up fading which has already occurred or an unsightly oil stain/cigarette burn, etc., which can't be easily removed. There are hundreds of styles and many different materials to choose from, so take your time and pick the right one.

SUN BLINDS
Another way to prevent the sun adversely affecting your interior trim is to fit and/or use sunblinds. Most resemble the domestic roller blind in operation. The base is screwed to a flat surface (usually the rear shelf) and then the blind can be pulled out and hooked open as required. Alternatives are a single-piece version which sticks onto the

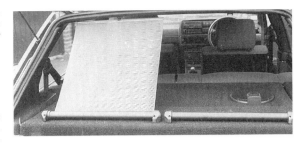

glass by means of suction caps and a similar model which retains the roller action of the permanent blinds. This is particularly useful for sticking onto a glass sunroof to prevent the high summer sun getting in the driver's eyes.

BEADY-EYED

On the same lines is the bead seat cover. Each one consists of hundreds of beads, strung together on strong nylon cords in such a way that they cover the seat backrest and squab. Again, elasticated straps and/or nylon ties are used. Though it will protect the seat to some extent, the actual aim is to offer a cooler, more comfortable ride. Considering the number sold some people must be finding it so, but it pays to try before you buy.

THE HOT SEAT

If you haven't got heated seats (a boon during the winter) you can fit an Otley heated cover, which plugs into the cigar lighter. It is fitted to the seat by elasticated straps around the backrest and squab.

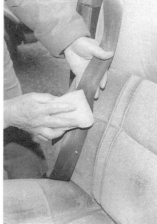

Far left: While you're working around the seats, check the seat belt mountings for security and the belts themselves along their length for damage.

Left: If they're OK, wash them with warm soapy water only - any chemicals could affect their efficiency.

Below: If you find problems, replacement is the only answer. Securon produce a wide range of original equipment standard belts.

❏ SEAT BELT CARE AND REPLACEMENT

SAFETY NOTE

You cannot repair seat belts; if you discover that a seat belt or mechanism is showing signs of wear or ageing, replace it straight away. The tips given here refer to standard seat belts and mechanisms. Some cars are fitted with more complex systems (pre-tensioners, etc.) in which case refer to the vehicle handbook for specific instructions.

CARING FOR SEAT BELTS

Taking care of your seat belts is something

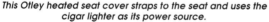

This Otley heated seat cover straps to the seat and uses the cigar lighter as its power source.

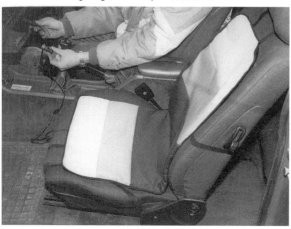

you can do every time you drive your car. Make sure that they are always retracted fully when not in use and are not left trapped for weeks on end (this applies particularly to rear seat belts).

Every now and again, pull all of the seat belt out and wipe it over with warm soapy water - but let it dry before retracting, though. Don't use anything of a harsh or chemical nature, as it might affect the belt's efficiency.

The buckle locking mechanisms and ratchets are also subject to wear and tear. Check that the belt releases quickly from the buckle and that the buckle is not rattling unduly.

Fitting tailored carpet mats will keep your carpets clean and protect them against wear and tear. (Courtesy Autostyle Unique)

Check also that the ratchet is locking the belt quickly when it is given a sharp tug and all the mounting bolts (including those of the buckles) are secure.

REPLACING BELTS

As already mentioned, damaged seat belts **CANNOT** be repaired. Replacing them is not a difficult task, nor is it particularly expensive. You can obtain new belts from your local dealer or from companies such as Securon, who produce a wide range of belts which are available from most major accessory stores.

All you need is a socket set and a torque wrench. The vital point is to make sure that you replace all those washers on the right bolts and in the right order - they're all there for a reason. Applying a blob of grease to the bolts as you replace them is always a good idea.

All seat belt anchor bolts should be tightened to a specific torque figure. This is something to check with the vehicle manufacturer or your local dealer.

❑ CARPET CLEANING

Most upholstery cleaners also work as carpet cleaners. In general, they are sprayed into the carpet and left to 'lift' the dirt out. When wiped with a damp cloth, the dirt emigrates to the cloth.

Renew upholstery cleaner works on headlinings and other trim items as well as carpets. Spray the foam on, work well into the carpet and sponge off. You can also use this product on most fabric seats.

Once they have thoroughly dried, you'll need to brush or vacuum the carpets once more until they're nice and clean. It is always advisable to fit loose protective floormats in your car, especially on the driver's side where the constant rubbing action of the heel (as the accelerator pedal is operated) can wear a hole in a surprisingly short time. It will help keep your original carpets clean and it's far cheaper to replace the odd mat than a complete front carpet section!

❑ STAIN REMOVAL GUIDE

Removing stains from the seats and carpets of your car can prove problematical, as there are different ways to deal with different stains. However, it's vital to remember to try out any 'remedy' on a small piece of out-of-the-way material/carpet first, in case it causes the colour to run or has a bleaching effect. This applies particularly when using proprietary cleaners with a solvent base. Always take great care when using cleaning chemicals of any description - many of them are highly dangerous when used incorrectly and/or inhaled. Make sure they are clearly labelled and stored safely.

BLOOD
When you get blood on your clothes, you soak them in biological washing powder, ideally overnight. Applying the same principle to, say, a car seat is somewhat difficult. However, you have to try and soak the stained area for as long as possible, using cold water - never warm or hot. An alternative is to use a dilution of cold water and ammonia. Whichever you choose, 'blot' rather than rub the stain out.

CHEWING GUM
There's an inevitability about children, cars and chewing gum and the best way to solve the problem is to ban gum, totally, from the car. If it's too late, then you should pull as much of it off the fabric as possible - don't rub it at all, you'll make it worse. Chewing gum is easier to manage when it's solid; to encourage this place a bag of ice cubes over it for a while, which will enable you to pick it off. You may need several applications and considerable patience to get the area totally gum-free.

MILK
If you spill milk in a car, you'll probably be crying over it before long - the resulting smell can be absolutely overpowering. This is the main reason that a milk spillage should be treated as a matter of urgency. Soak up the milk as much as possible with a sponge or a cloth and then use a proprietary carpet/upholstery cleaner on the affected areas. If the smell remains, wipe over with a water/ammonia mixture.

OIL
If you work on your own car, it's highly likely that oil will at some point find its way onto your upholstery. Use cotton wool soaked in carbon tetrachloride to dab the stain away and then use a standard carpet cleaner. You may not be able to get to the very heart of the stain, in which case the oil/grease will tend to 'rise again' whereupon you should repeat the above operation.

TAR
Many companies market a tar remover, though you must be careful that you don't just dilute the tar and make things worse by spreading it around. Use an absorbent cloth to 'blot' the stain out, or even a piece of blotting paper. Alternatively, eucalyptus oil, available from most chemists, works well. Finish off by wiping the area with a mixture of hot water and washing powder/liquid.

TEA / COFFEE
If the stain is still wet, mop up the excess and treat the area with a borax/warm water solution. Where the stain has been allowed to dry for any length of time, apply a 50/50 solution of water and glycerine and leave for about an hour. Sponge off and then treat the area with a proprietary cleaner

VOMIT
An unpleasant subject, but a fact of life, as people and animals suffer from travel sickness. Sponge the area with water/carpet cleaner/disinfectant solution. For stubborn marks, clean with a solution of washing powder in water and then sponge off using clean water.

❏ REPAIRING INTERIOR TRIM
CLOTH SEATS
If you've got seats covered in woven fabric, the best way to repair a hole in a cloth seat is to get weaving - literally! You'll need a needle and some strong thread that's a good match for the seat colour. In most cases, the repair is best effected with the seat out of the car - indoors where you can control the light is probably best. The diagrams illustrate how a woven repair should be carried out: there should be a large area of overlap around the hole to prevent future fraying, and the stitches going from side to side (the warps) should not be pulled tight but left quite loose. This is because the up and down stitches which follow (the wefts) are going to 'weave' inside them - hence the name. With a little practice, you should be able to make an almost invisible mend. This technique can also be used on other items of interior cloth trim, door panel inserts, for example.

VINYL SEATS
Vinyl does not lend itself to woven repairs,

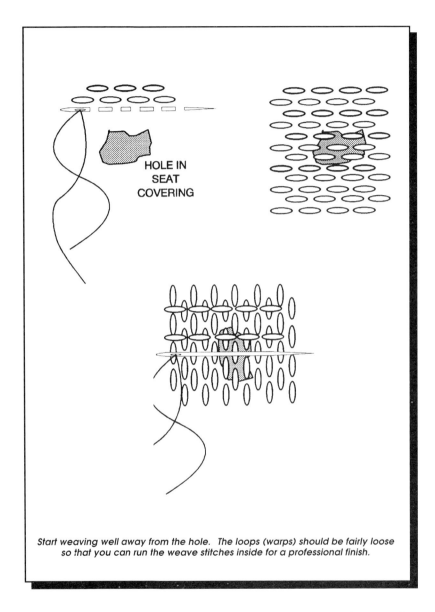

Start weaving well away from the hole. The loops (warps) should be fairly loose so that you can run the weave stitches inside for a professional finish.

so different tactics have to be employed. Where the seat has a small rip, use Loctite's Vinyl Bond to glue the sides of the rip together again. This specialist glue works by literally melting the pieces of vinyl together, rather like a weld.

Use a fine grade sandpaper to roughen the edges of the tear. Once you've applied the glue to both sides, it needs to be held in place for about an hour - use masking tape along the top to do this. When the tape is removed, the join should be permanent. Any excess glue can be removed by careful sanding.

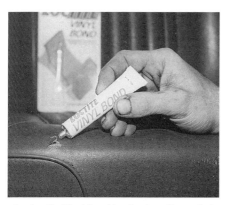

Use Loctite Vinyl Bond to glue together a rip in the seat or trim panel.

Where the rip is bigger, you'll need to cut a piece of material larger than the rip and insert underneath the seat covering. The two sides of the rip are then glued to the new piece. It needs to be left for a while to set properly, preferably overnight. To help keep the sides in place masking tape should be used.

SPLIT SEAMS
You can use your sewing skills again if you have a seat with a split seam. Use a curved needle and start the repair slightly before the split. Many seat materials are thick enough to cause real problems with getting the needle through; take care not to hurt yourself with the needle - use a pair of pliers to pull it through.

With tough materials, such as leather and some fabrics, you may be able to pass the needle and thread through the existing holes. If the holes have worn or frayed, it's best to make new ones.

DAMAGED CARPETS
If you find a rip in your carpet, you can repair it in the same way you would a household carpet. If it's practical, remove the carpet from the car. If the damage is just a rip or tear, use domestic carpet repair tape along the back. This is extremely strong stuff which is unlikely to allow the rip to open further.

A larger damaged area calls for more ingenuity, as you'll have to remove a section and replace it with fresh carpet. You may be able to pick up a piece of carpet from a scrap car - look especially in the boot, where the carpet gets far less wear. Alternatively, a local trim specialist (or even local dealer) may supply you with a small piece of carpet. As a last resort, you could even 'steal' a piece of carpet from the boot of your own car - out of the way, of course, where it won't show.

Use a craft knife and cut a section of the original away, making straight lines and allowing about 1 inch all round. Take this piece to your replacement carpet section and cut a piece to match exactly.

Stick domestic carpet repair tape onto the underside of the original and then lay the patch down on top where it will stick into position. If you've been accurate in your cutting, it should be exact. At first, there will be a colour difference, but shampoo the whole area and within a couple of weeks it will be barely detectable.

HEADLININGS
If there's a rip in your car's vinyl headlining, the basic repair techniques are the same as for repairing vinyl trim and seats. The obvious problem is that you can't apply pressure from the underside of the headlining. All you can do is glue the edges as usual and hold together as best you can. If your headlining is the perforated variety, you may be able to insert a needle through one of them at one side of the rip and out at the other, thus giving something to press against. If the rip is a long one (2 or 3 inches) it's best to tackle it in several separate stages rather than trying to complete the repair in one go.

If the damaged headlining is cloth, use a curved needle (as per the seat repair) to sew up the rip.

CIGARETTE BURNS
The most common cause of damaged seats is a cigarette burn. The heat from the cigarette usually causes the hole to seal itself and thus prevent any possibility of it spreading. But it's still unsightly and could be a bargaining point when it comes to selling the car.

The easiest way to repair it is to cut a small piece of fabric from the underside of the seat, or possibly under the rear seats. If there's a 'grain' to the covering, make sure you get it right, otherwise it will stand out as much as the hole you're trying to cover up!

marked by a cigarette burn, carefully scrape away the blackened area and use a small brush to apply bleach to it. This will gradually bring the colour back to the wood. Use a wood dye to get it exactly right.

Cut a neat piece which will overlap the hole and, ideally, butt up with a natural join, *e.g.* the seams. Using the new piece as a template, mark its size on the area in question and remove a piece of suitable size from the seat. By using the correct glue, the new piece will stick neatly into place and, with a little time to 'weather in', will be hard to spot.

Where the cigarette has scorched but not burned the trim right through, it can sometimes be rectified. If it's not too badly damaged, try rubbing the area with a water/borax solution. If this doesn't work, try a solution of hydrogen peroxide and water; **CAUTION**, this is a strong chemical and you should test it on a hidden piece of trim for adverse reactions before applying to the stain.

REPAIRING VINYL TRIM

If you have a rip in a vinyl-covered trim panel, it can be repaired in the same way as a seat; small rips require sanding down and then a dab of Loctite vinyl mender. Larger rips should be secured underneath with masking tape before applying the Loctite.

If you have a scuff mark or very small area of damage on a trim panel, it's often possible to 'cheat' - take a suitably coloured felt tip pen and apply it to the area bereft of vinyl.

WOODEN TRIM REPAIR TIPS

• If you have wooden trim which is

• Where you have a stubborn mark or stain on wooden trim, rub the area with equal parts of linseed oil and cleaning fluid, then wipe off.

• Dents in wood can usually be removed by placing a wet cloth over the affected area and then applying a hot iron - safety must be uppermost in your mind here. The steam produced will cause the wood to swell, though it may take more than one application to bring the dent out totally.

• You can fill a depression or damaged area of wooden trim using 'plastic wood' available from most DIY stores. Some types absorb varnish/stain, others retain their colour. You want the former.

• An alternative is to melt a stick of coloured Shellac into the depression. This is available from craft shops or furniture restoration specialists.

• If you have a problem with blistered wood veneer, try this; carefully cut along the blister with a sharp knife (watch those fingers!) and then squeeze PVA adhesive into the cut. It's a fiddly job, so take your time. Cover the blister with blotting paper and aluminium foil and secure it in place using masking tape. Apply a heat source - a hot air gun or domestic iron and, at the same time, press on the area with something flat - your sanding block, for example. (It's a good idea to wear a thick glove to protect the hand that's doing the pressing). You'll only need to heat for around a minute, but keep the pressure on until the

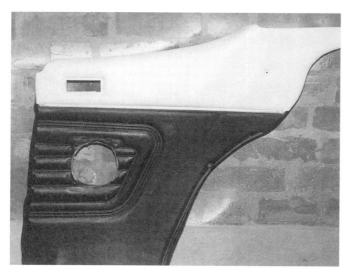

This door trim was black. The top half has already been sprayed white and, once dry...

... was masked-off and the lower half sprayed light brown.

area has cooled and the glue set.

❑ PAINTING INTERIOR TRIM

When your interior trim gets so dirty it can't be cleaned (or when you just fancy a change) there are now a number of paints available in a range of colours. You can spray your door trims, dashboard or even your car's leather or vinyl seats if you wish!

Most 'plastic' paints work by penetrating the surface of the material down to

the substrata, where it bonds itself to the molecules and changes the pigmentation. In plain English, this means that it can't flake off! Many can be used on leather as well as vinyl and, because it's not really a paint (though it's simpler to refer to it as such), it doesn't cover grain in either material. If required, leather trim can still be 'fed' with hide food and, of course, the lovely aroma remains.

To a great extent, spraying interior trim is

like spraying a body panel, though of course, you don't have to take anti-rust precautions. The trim panels should be removed from the car and thoroughly cleaned. Any pieces of brightwork or items such as an integral ashtray, should be removed. The surface to be sprayed should be rubbed over lightly with a rag dipped in cellulose thinners - too much will cause vinyl to melt. If, as shown in the photos here, you are going for a two-tone effect,

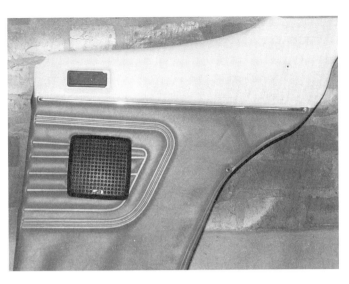

The finished item, with all the trim fittings replaced. The 'paint' permeates the vinyl and changes the colour from within - it won't flake off.

you'll need to mask-off as shown in Chapter 10.

Heed the usual rules of aerosol spraying (Chapter 10 again) and apply several light coats rather than trying to complete the job in one go.

If you're doing a lot of trim (changing the colour of the whole interior, for example) it may be worth buying the paint in large cans and using a proprietary spray gun. A small one like the Humbrol model shown here will do a lot of work for little capital outlay.

As always, consider where the over-spray is going to go and mask-off the surrounding area as required.

DEALING WITH LEAKS
HOW TO KEEP WATER OUT OF YOUR CAR

Water leaking into the car can create a multitude of problems. If it gets into the electrical system, it can cause short circuits resulting in breakdowns, possible damage to equipment, or even a fire. If it drips into a place where it can sit undisturbed, it could be the cause of rust damage and if it drips onto carpet or interior trim you end up with mildew or rot. Plenty of reasons to sort out a leak, pronto!

❏ FINDING THE SOURCE
Usually it's fairly obvious where the water is coming in, though on odd occasions some detective work is required. Water could, for example, be coming into the car via a rusty hole in, say, the underside of the wing - a hole not visible because it is hidden by a piece of cracked underseal.

If you believe it to be coming through a leak in the glass weather sealing strip, sit in the car and have a helper hose it down, paying particular attention to the suspect area. With a little luck, you'll be able to see where the water is coming in. If you can't see it, but still believe the rubber is leaking, use chalk dust along the rubber; the leaking water will wash it away at the entry point.

❏ STEMMING THE TIDE
Leaking rubbers around glass can be sealed by using a proprietary sealant. Pull back the weatherstrip and squirt in the sealant, which will flow into the affected area.

It could be that the water is coming in because of a leaking weatherstrip on a door or hatch/boot. An examination may show instantly where the problem lies, for example, when it has seriously deteriorated or where pieces of rubber are missing. If

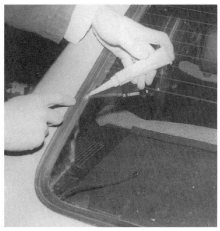

Use Loctite's Clear Silicone Sealant or Comma's Seek 'n' Seal to solve leaking glass rubber seal problems.

not, use the hose pipe/chalk dust routine again.

It may be possible to reseal the weatherstrip using the products mentioned earlier, though it is in the nature of rubber to harden and crack with age. Eventually, it gets to a point where the only solution is to replace the weatherstrip.

If you've checked all the obvious possibilities but water is still getting into the car or boot, consider the windscreen wiper spindles (should be protected by waterproof grease), heater intake areas (usually have rubber drain tubes), aerial base, number-plate and badge fixings which pass through the bodywork. Also, if your car is fitted with an electric sunroof, check that its drain tubes are clear.

LOCKS AND LATCHES
MAINTENANCE AND GENERAL ADVICE

In general, your car's door locks are unlikely to give you much trouble; most problems are caused by neglect which is a shame, really, as they take so little looking after. All they need is a drop of oil and/or a smidgen of grease every now and again and they'll go on forever. Apart from the obvious inconvenience of not being able to lock/

Looking after your locks takes no time at all - spray in WD40 to keep them operational and trouble-free.

Door, bonnet and boot latches benefit from a smear of copper-based grease every now and then.

unlock a door, there's the fact that door latching (which includes the boot or hatchback tailgate) is now an MoT testable item.

❏ CENTRAL LOCKING

Central locking tends to be more problematical. Systems are either pneumatic or electronic in operation, with most cars featuring the latter (companies such as Mercedes and Audi favour the quieter pneumatic version) and any aftermarket central locking kit is almost certain to be electronic in operation. Most use the driver's door lock as a master with the others in the system being slaves.

When the driver's side lock is operated, all the others follow on. In the case of pneumatic locks, the action of the key in the driver's door operates a pneumatic pump (usually situated out of the way in the boot); in an electric system, it triggers a switch in a central control module which passes the electronic order on to the rest of the locks.

In all systems, each door* is equipped with a small motor which operates the on/off control - locked or unlocked.

If you've got old-fashioned locking knobs like these, you can improve your car's security by sawing off the tops and making them hard to grip by a thief's wire hook.

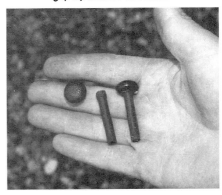

There's always plenty of wiring with electric central locking. Check integrity of connections and general continuity when fault finding.

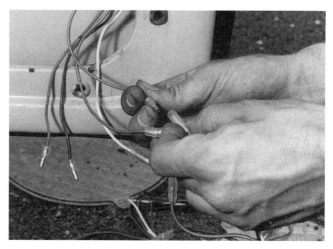

* On some systems, the driver's door does not feature a motor - in these cases, one is necessary in order to add central locking to an alarm system.

❑ ELECTRIC LOCKING FAULT FINDING

If your car's central locking system isn't working, check that the fuses are OK and that the locking motors are receiving power. There are usually plenty of wires around and it's easy for them to come adrift. Check by removing the door trim panels.

Another common problem is that the rods linking the motors to the original locks work loose and/or come off altogether. Again, removing the trim and having a look is the answer. Whilst you're in there, break out the Waxoyl and give the inner door some rust protection - see Chapter 11.

❑ PNEUMATIC LOCKING FAULT FINDING

With a pneumatic system similar checks can be made. The air is passed around the car via lengths of plastic piping which can get trapped, come off the connections or simply perish with age. Finding a problem pipe is a matter of plodding detective work. It's rare that a damaged pipe can be repaired. In addition, the pump itself is often a source of (expensive) grief. It usually signals its impending demise by being increasingly tardy in unlocking the doors.

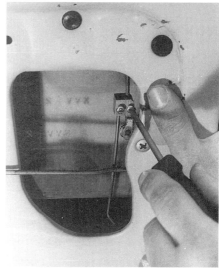

Many locking systems use rods and screw-type clamp blocks to link into the original mechanism. These can work loose over the years.

ENGINE BAY VALETING
HOW TO GET THE ENGINE BAY REALLY CLEAN

So, you've got the cleanest, sparkling, most eye-catching motor on the mews; the paintwork shines with a mirror-like finish and the wax is deep enough to drown in. But when you lift the bonnet - oh dear; the space where the engine should be looks like the aftermath of the Amoco Cadiz oil spillage!

For many, lifting the bonnet is a bit like paying income tax - it's only done when absolutely necessary and then not with good grace. The resulting oily, dirty mess is not only unsightly, it's potentially dangerous and could leave you stranded.

How? Well, consider that metal cars (or cars with a metal chassis) are all subject to the rigours of rust. Some more than others, but the principle holds true. Just as you can't see what lies beneath a layer of road dirt stuck to the exterior bodywork, neither can you see what nasties lurk beneath that thick covering of grime in the engine compartment. An area of surface rust could easily have become a dangerous hole and a slight crack a large one.

Moreover, engines are meant to be clean; HT leads, for example, do not perform at their best when covered in a layer of oil and dirt, particularly the latter which attracts moisture and can cause shorting-out problems.

❏ WATER IN THE WORKS
Unless you've got a diesel engine under the bonnet (in which case you're allowed a smug grin) you'll have to take precautions to avoid getting water into the engine's electrical system.

Use a plastic bag and rubber band to cover the top of the distributor and spray all HT leads with a moisture repellent before you go mad with the hose. (Note that the rust preventative, Waxoyl, can be used in this way.) Also cover fuse boxes, alternator/dynamo, starter motor and the top of the dipstick.

❏ WAX
If you've got a car which came from the factory with the engine bay covered in wax, you face a dilemma - clearly the wax is left there to prevent the onset of rust but, equally, it attracts dirt and oil and makes the engine bay a very messy place to be.
It's your choice!

❏ OIL
The biggest single cause of mess in the engine bay is oil in its various forms. Not only is it dirty in itself, it also means that

Spray-on de-greasant is the easiest way to spruce up your engine bay. Protect electrics with plastic bags while you rinse off with lots of water. Use a stiff brush where the dirt/grease is particularly stubborn When painting under-bonnet items, use a high-heat paint and apply the usual rules of spraying.

When painting under-bonnet items, use a high-heat paint and apply the usual rules of spraying.

❏ SPRAYING OFF

The de-greasant dissolves the oily mess and can be washed off with water. Again, you might need to encourage the dirt to leave with that stiff brush. Bear in mind that the resultant water and oil river you'll create is particularly messy - don't do the job on your newly-paved driveway.

❏ PAINTING UNDER THE BONNET

As well as cleaning under the bonnet, you can apply imagination and paint to brighten things up a little. There are many companies which produce high-heat spray paints in a wide range of colours. These, as you can guess, are designed to stand up to quite incredible temperatures and can be used on items like exhaust manifolds, rocker covers, radiator surrounds and cylinder heads, etc. Preparation mirrors that of bodywork painting, in that the item to be covered should be clean and grease-free. Sand down and mask-off where appropriate, heeding the general rules of aerosol spraying (see Chapter 10).

road dirt, etc., sticks to it. Though it does tend to inhibit corrosion, you still can't see what's going on underneath - and you need to. What you need, then, is a de-greasant. There are plenty on the market, most of which are now available in non-aerosol spray bottles. Unlike wax (where you have to be careful where you spray it) you can blast away with some vigour with this under the bonnet. Make sure you get into all the awkward little corners and it's also a good idea to work it into the oily grime using a stiff brush. I usually use the one designed for alloy wheel cleaning as it is up to the job and nifty enough to get where other brushes can't.